2nd Edition

MANAGING
A PROGRAMMING
PROJECT

PHILIP W. METZGER

PRENTICE-HALL, INC., Englewood Cliffs, New Jersey 07632

Library of Congress Cataloging in Publication Data

Metzger, Philip W
   Managing a programming project.
   Bibliography: p. 239
   Includes index.
    1. Electronic digital computers — Programming.
2. Computer programming management. I. Title.
QA76.6.M47 1981   001.64'2   80-26327
ISBN 0-13-550772-3

Editorial/production supervision
  and interior design by *Linda Mihatov Paskiet*
Cover design by *Jorge Hernandez*
Manufacturing buyers: *Joyce Levatino*
  and Gordon Osbourne

Printed in the United States of America

10 9

PRENTICE-HALL INTERNATIONAL, INC., *London*
PRENTICE-HALL OF AUSTRALIA PTY. LIMITED, *Sydney*
PRENTICE-HALL OF CANADA, LTD., *Toronto*
PRENTICE-HALL OF INDIA PRIVATE LIMITED, *New Delhi*
PRENTICE-HALL OF JAPAN, INC., *Tokyo*
PRENTICE-HALL OF SOUTHEAST ASIA PTE. LTD., *Singapore*
WHITEHALL BOOKS LIMITED, *Wellington, New Zealand*

Contents

The Manager's Job *129*

Technical leadership 129; Planning and controlling 131;
Communicating 131; Carrying the water 132;
Assigning the work 134; Working hours 135;
Adding more people 136; Reporting technical status 137;
Reporting financial status 140; Training 140;
Appraising and counseling 142; Sanity maintenance 143;
First-level vs. upper-level management 145

Chapter 5 **The System Test Phase** **146**

System Testing *146*

System test specification 147; The testers 149; Timing 150;
Conducting the tests 152

Customer Training *153*

Using the system 153; Maintaining the system 154

Chapter 6 **The Acceptance Phase** **155**

Acceptance Testing *155*

Acceptance test specification 155; Acceptance criteria 156;
Execution 158

Documentation *158*

Chapter 7 **The Installation and Operation Phase** **160**

Site Testing *160*
Conversion *161*

Parallel operation 161; Immediate replacement 162;
Cutover 162

Maintenance And Tuning *163*
Project Evaluation *163*

Chapter 8 **Special Considerations** **165**

Big Projects *165*

The phases 166; Organization 168; Customer controls 169;
Configuration management 170; Multiple releases 172

Small Projects *173*
Proposals *174*

Chapter 9 **A War Story** **177**

New kid on the job 177; Project status 179;
Your background 180; Your job 181; Five months later 181;
Current situation 184; Happy New Year 185; Epilogue 187

List of Illustrations

Preface

When this book was first published in 1973 it was structured around a basic concept called a development cycle: an orderly series of events in the life of a programming project. Because that concept is as valid today as ever, I have retained it in this revision. What has changed significantly, however, is the set of tools and techniques used during the various stages of the cycle. Concepts such as top-down development and structured programming, for example, were little understood and certainly not universally accepted in 1973; they are now a part of the management lore.

As for writing style, I have tried to retain a fairly informal tone, as in the original book. I don't want you to snore after three paragraphs. I have offered guidelines, but have not included the huge volume of theory and data available to support them. That's available from many other sources, including the excellent writings listed in the Bibliography and References section.

A final note: One of the things that changed for the better during the 70s was the recognition of women as equals (at least!) in the computer business world as in everything else. Some of my reviewers did not like my use of "he" where "he or she" is really meant. I have used words such as "person," where possible, to include and be fair to both sexes. But I still balk at constructions such as "he/she" or "person-months." Sorry. No chauvinism intended.

For the Teacher

A Management Instruction Package is now available from the author. This teaching guide is based on *Managing a Programming Project*, Second Edition. Its contents include: I Introduction; II General Course Outline; III Detailed Course Outline; IV Visual Aids; V Case Study; VI Class Problem; VII Conducting the Class.

For further information, write to:

Philip W. Metzger
5613 Old National Pike
Frederick, MD 21701

PHILIP METZGER

ACKNOWLEDGMENTS

This book is the result of ideas gathered during my own experience as a programmer, manager, staff assistant, and instructor. More important than my own direct experience, however, is what I've picked up through long association with many technicians and managers in the programming field, some of them the best in the business. It's impossible to mention and thank everyone who helped me in various ways, but there are several whose contributions I'd like specifically to acknowledge.

First, thanks to Joel Aron and Al Pietrasanta. Both of their successful careers in IBM have embraced every kind of assignment from technical to managerial, with teaching and staff jobs in between. Joel and Al were responsible for creating a popular series of programming management classes in IBM. It was after attending one of these classes and then taking over responsibility myself for those same classes within IBM's Federal Systems Division that I first began writing the notes that led to the first version of this book. Both Joel and Al have been extremely generous in giving me the freedom to draw upon and extend the work they began. In addition, Joel did a most thorough and very helpful review of the manuscript for this revised edition. In some instances he saved me from some serious blunders.

Next, thanks to Roy Heistand and Jim Greenwood, two senior managers at IBM who encouraged me to get out the first edition of the book; Roy was directly responsible for my association with editor Karl Karlstrom of Prentice-Hall, who in turn has been most helpful and encouraging. Without his gentle prodding, I never would have gotten at this revision.

Roy Klaskin, another friend and senior manager in IBM, reviewed both the original and this revised manuscript, and offered a bushel of suggestions for correcting and improving the book. Like Joel, Roy has had a long career embracing not only actual programming, but management on several levels, staff assignments, and teaching. At one point in his career he was even a judge!

My thanks to two gentlemen who came from out of nowhere one day to *volunteer* to review the manuscript for this edition: Larry Holland and Paul Guinzburg, the senior staff of Software Implementation, Inc., located in Fort Lee, New Jersey. While their act of volunteering leaves their sanity somewhat in doubt, I am very grateful for their many suggestions. Since they have extensive experience in commercial data processing, they helped balance my own government-oriented background. Paul and Larry are deeply involved in *teaching* software management techniques, among other things, and had used the first edition of my book for class reading; when they found I was doing a revision, they wanted me to get it right this time!

Next, thanks to Shirley Porter, who has no credentials in programming but who read the manuscript to see if it made sense from a layman's point-of-view, helped me through the labor of proofreading, corrected my spelling, and kept me at the job.

And finally, I bow with respect and appreciation in the direction of Linda Paskiet of Prentice-Hall, who somehow organized and made sense of my sloppy manuscript. I never would have believed a clean book could emerge from all that mess!

My sincere thanks to all!

To Shirley

Part I

THE PROGRAMMING DEVELOPMENT CYCLE

Chapter I

Introduction

Since the first edition of this book was published in 1973, much has changed in the computer business. Computers have become smaller, more powerful, and dramatically cheaper. There have been other changes, potentially even more significant in their impact on computer usage, but not as visible. These changes have to do with the way the beasts are programmed and managed. During the 1970s there was feverish activity among computer scientists and practicing programmers seeking new methods of producing good programs, on time and more efficiently.

During the 1980s the search continues, but a good many projects are already immersed in some of the "new" methodologies, such as structured programming and top-down development. Before long, reliable programs, produced within the limitations of a budget and on time, will no longer be a rarity, although it will take some time before they become an everyday occurrence.

Managers during the 1980s are faced with some fundamental decisions which were not so much in evidence during prior decades. Some of these decisions go to the very core of programming and affect everything the manager does from his first day on the project, including how he organizes his people, what kinds of talent he must find, how computer testing time should be spaced, and, in fact, how he defines the development cycle for the project. In the following chapters I will point out some of the choices a manager must make and give some guidance to help make those choices.

THE MANAGEMENT BUSINESS

A manager's job is to plan an activity and then see that it is carried out. But from the instant the project begins, he must contend with the fact that humans tend not to solve problems until they become crises. Only a crisis seems worthy of real attention, given the many demands on our time. Whether it's a strike deadline, an international diplomatic standoff, a human injustice, or a clogged sewer, nothing gets resolved until something overflows. Book revisions don't get written until the deadline is two months away. And of course, computer programs don't get serious attention until the deadline is terrifyingly close at hand or the customer is threatening to sue! It's practically a law: a problem must reach crisis proportions before we act to solve it.

On computer programming projects there is a common scenario: time passes and problems develop. Everybody knows it but the status charts are "fudged" in the name of optimism. (We'll make up the lost time next month.) But more time passes and managers begin to feel queasy. An important delivery date arrives and there's nothing to deliver. Mild panic. Meetings. When *will* the item be delivered, Mr. Manager? Next month. No question about it. We've put Charlie Superprogrammer on the job.

But Charlie turns out to be human; next month arrives, and still no product. Another cycle or two and in comes the Company-Vice-President-In-Charge-Of-Boondoggles. He'll fix things with his heavy hammer. But that doesn't work either.

Finally, a high-level decision is made to stop, take stock, and come up with a new plan for finishing. New plan? Ah, there's the rub. Quite likely it will be the first plan.

Well, why not plan really well in the first place? You'll end up having to do it sooner or later. If you do it sooner, you'll keep the Vice-President out of your hair. If you do it later, plan on hypertension, ulcers, and overruns.

The aim of this book is to get you, the manager, to *plan*, and then *control* your project according to that plan. Almost any plan is better than none at all. You really have a clear choice: plan now and enjoy a successful project, or order yourself a space in the management graveyard.

ABOUT THIS BOOK

I am addressing you, the reader, as if you were the manager of a medium-sized programming project involving about forty people —

programmers, managers, and others. Larger and smaller projects are discussed in Chapter 8. If your project is very small, please don't toss the book aside and snort that you don't need all that stuff for your six-person job. Most of what you'll read here is vital regardless of project size. What varies from one job to the next is not what tasks you need to do, but how much horsepower you need to do them.

The title "manager" means different things to different organizations. I use it to identify those people who are responsible for planning and directing the implementation of some job, and who have direct responsibility for hiring and firing, adjusting salaries, and promotions. A *first-level manager* has the closest supervision over the people who actually build the product; a second-level manager supervises first-level managers, and so on. In many organizations the term "supervisor" replaces what I have called a first-level manager. Sometimes the two titles are synonymous, but more often the supervisor gives technical direction without having direct responsibility for hiring, firing, salary, and promotions; however, supervisors do have plenty of influence in all those areas.

In this book the terms *program* and *software* are synonymous. *Operational programs* are those written to do the job for which your project exists, e.g., calculating payroll checks, directing space flights, producing management reports. *Support programs* are those utilized as aids in producing the operational programs.

This book is divided into two parts. Part I describes what should happen on a well-behaved project; Part II outlines a planning document (the Project Plan) essential to good management. After reading Part I you'll find Part II immediately useful as a model for your own project's plan.

ESTABLISH YOUR GROUND RULES

As you read the literature you may easily despair of the diverse and often contradictory definitions and uses of terms such as software, module, integration, system test, and so on.

One day, when The Computer takes control, He will straighten out the whole mess and send down a printout defining everything clearly and unambiguously. From that day forth, all programming people shall speak a common tongue. Until that time, while we're still groping, trying, testing, the best we can do is decide that *now*, *for this project*, *these* are the definitions we will use and *this* is the management scheme we will follow. Don't fret if this does not conform to the "right" way of doing things; there is no single "right" way, but only alternatives from which we must choose. Don't drift. Consistency within a project will contribute immensely toward a successful project. Here are some ground rules to establish:

- Define your project's *development cycle* and relate all schedules and activities to that cycle. This book is built around one such development cycle. When I mention, say, the *Programming Phase*, you may be assured that I always mean a certain time slice one can point to on a simple chart, and there are always certain activities associated with that phase. Don't call it the "Programming Phase" in one breath and the "Implementation Phase" in the next. It doesn't matter, of course, what names you choose; just be consistent.

- Define *activities*, such as levels of testing, in a consistent way. Until there is a universally accepted set of definitions, adopt those that make sense to you, and stick with them. In this book, for instance, I define system testing in a certain way; other books use that term for what I call integration test. Too bad, but at least know what *you* on your project mean and be sure everyone else does, too.

- Define a *system of documents* clearly, consistently, and early. Then hang anyone who operates outside that system. There will be enough paperwork on any project without the headache of random documents that can't be controlled and whose authority is suspect. I've seen plenty of wheel-spinning by people confronted with a new set of paper somebody had decided to call "specifications," but which were really random programmers' thoughts on random subjects.

- In summary, define the development process for your project, believe in it, sell it to your people, and enforce it.

YOUR CONTRACT

What do you mean, you don't have a contract! If you don't, you're already in trouble. Half the horror stories about programming involve either bad contracts or no contract at all.

A contract is an agreement between you and a customer that you will do a certain job within specific constraints for so much money. Don't operate on the basis of verbal agreements or casual memos, even if your customer happens to be your buddy down the hall and you both work for the same organization. Within your company, you may call your document a "letter of understanding" or something similar which sounds friendlier than "contract." In any case, you need a formal written statement clearly showing what the customer wants and what you agree to provide. Operating without such an agreement is lunacy for both parties, as many a programming manager and just as many customers have found out.

If your organization is small, and you have no formal way of dealing with contracts, you can write one yourself to cover the essentials:

1. *Scope of work.* What is the job to be done? If the job definition is too vague, maybe you need two contracts: one to define the job and one to write programs.

2. *Schedule and deliverables.* What specific items (programs, documents) are to be delivered to the customer? When are they to be delivered? Where are they to be delivered? In what form (card decks, tapes, diskettes; drafts or clean documents)? How many copies?

3. *Key people.* Who is authorized to approve changes and accept the finished product?

4. *Review schedule.* When and how shall the customer be given reviews and reports of progress? What is required of the customer if he disapproves of a report?

5. *Change control procedures.* What will be the mechanism for dealing with items the customer demands which you consider changes to the original work scope?

6. *Testing constraints.* Where and under whose control will computer or other test time be obtained? During which work shifts? Exactly what priority will your programmers have?

7. *Acceptance criteria.* What are the specific quantitative criteria to be used in judging whether your finished product is acceptable?

8. *Any additional constraints.* Are there items which may be peculiar to your working environment? Are you to use customer personnel? If so, what control do you have over them? Are there special data security problems? Is the customer required to supply test data? If so, what kinds of data, in what form, when, and how clean?

9. *Price.* What is your price for doing the job? Is it fixed or variable? If variable, under what circumstances?

All of these items and more will be addressed in much more detail throughout the book. The last item, price, is handled in a good many different ways, depending on the type of contract agreed upon. Here is a brief summary of formal contract types.

Firm Fixed Price (FFP)

The price is set and not subject to change even if you have estimated badly. This is the most risky type of contract to use on a programming job. It should *never* be used without at least a very clear statement of work, no fuzzy areas, no dangling definitions. Many a project has experienced severe losses operating under such a contract.

Fixed Price with Escalation (FP-E)

The price is set, but some allowance is made for both upward and downward adjustments in case certain things happen, for example, labor rates or material costs change.

Fixed Price Incentive (FPI)

A target price is set, but formulas are established that allow the contractor a higher percentage of profit if he exceeds selected targets, such as cost, and a lower percentage of profit (even a loss) if he misses the targets.

Cost Shared

This type of contract reimburses the contractor for part or all of his costs but allows no profit, or fee. It's used either for research work with nonprofit organizations or in joint projects between the customer and the contractor where there is anticipated benefit to the contractor. For example, the job may result in a product which the contractor will have the exclusive right to sell.

Cost Plus Incentive Fee (CPIF)

This provides that the contractor will be paid all his costs plus a fee which varies depending on how close the contractor comes to meeting the established target costs, or how well he does in other areas spelled out in the contract. A variation is Cost Plus Award Fee (CPAF). In the case of CPIF, the criteria which determine the fee are all objective and measureable; in CPAF, the criteria are more subjective and are weighed by a board of review.

Cost Plus Fixed Fee (CPFF)

The contractor is paid allowable costs and a set fee.

Time & Materials (T&M)

Here the contractor is paid for labor hours actually worked and the cost of materials used.

Labor Hour

Labor hours are paid for, but nothing else.

The last two contract types are pretty much risk-free for the contractor. He provides people to do as the customer directs. The other contract types involve varying degrees of risk for the contractor and the customer. When the deliverable product can be well defined in advance, the contractor may propose a fixed price and a high fee. When the end product is poorly defined or subject to change, a cost type of contract is appropriate, from the contractor's point of view. His profit is lower, but so is his risk.

TOP-DOWN DEVELOPMENT

Traditionally, most programs have been analyzed and designed top-down, and coded and tested from the bottom up. During analysis and design it seemed natural to start by first considering the system as a whole and then to break it down into smaller and smaller pieces which individuals could handle. Then the pieces were coded and tested, and combined ("integrated") into increasingly larger and more complex groupings until finally the entire system had been assembled from the bottom up.

Many systems are still being built that way. But the trend is toward complete top-down development, wherein not only analysis and design are attacked from the top, but so are coding and integration testing. The approach I recommend in the following pages is top-down development, but I've described both approaches in order that you might make a reasoned decision about which way to go on your own project.

AN ATYPICAL PROJECT

Chapter 9 suggests what may go awry by using the story of an actual project beset by problems as an example. It's a fairly typical situation. Here I'd like to do the opposite: describe briefly a well-run and successful project — unfortunately, not so typical.

A programming project begins with an idea some user has about a need the computer might handle. The user solicits ideas from associates and contractors about the reasonableness of the idea and possible embellishments. After some incubation and revision, the now firmer idea is formally submitted, usually to competing contractors, for bids. The competitors jump into feverish activity called proposal writing. Each tries to figure how he can meet this user's needs at lower cost and with better quality than the others are likely to propose. Each writes a statement of his understanding of the problem and how he would solve it with computer programs. Each adds a layer of boilerplate to try to impress the customer with his credentials, and the proposals are submitted for evaluation.

Of the contenders considered responsive to his needs, the customer selects one, usually the lowest bidder, to do the job. If none are responsive enough, he redefines the requirements and asks for new proposals.

The winner celebrates his good fortune while the losers applaud, and the project begins. The winner appoints a project manager who organizes a team (partly kept in readiness since the proposals were first submitted) to do this job.

The team tackles two immediate tasks: one is to define in clear detail the customer's needs, the other is to write a plan for filling those needs. Both tasks were "done" during the proposal stage, but now they must be refined. A very precise, structured problem description document must be written to serve as the baseline for subsequent design and programming; and a detailed plan, minus the public-relations boilerplate, must be written to guide all the remaining phases of the project.

That accomplished, the project manager must recruit and organize the talent needed for the next phase: designing the program system. He selects the very best designers he can, including some of the analysts, and directs them to design the best possible program system to match the problem defined by the analysts. While design is going on the project manager is busy recruiting people and finding other resources, such as computer time, for the remaining work to be done. He keeps his eye on the project's plan and takes steps to meet all the milestones stated in it. Sometimes he sees a need to change the plan, and he does so.

When the overall program system design is ready, it's reviewed and approved by project management and the customer, established as the baseline for detailed design and coding, and turned over to the programmers.

Programmers further refine the baseline design into smaller pieces, until the refinements reach the level of actual code. The pieces ("modules") are coded and tested and carefully merged ("integrated") with one another in a preplanned manner. As modules are added successfully, the program system grows in complexity and usefulness. It reaches a number of plateaus where it can be shown to be performing some subset of its intended functions. Because design integrity was sought and achieved in earlier phases, the system fits together well. Yet there will be analysis, design, or coding mistakes. Changes are made as necessary, but they are strictly controlled through a simple mechanism earlier planned for.

Finally, the program system is ready for the customer, along with its set of descriptive documentation and a set of draft user documentation. But the customer doesn't yet get his hands on the product. First it's wrung out through another set of tests called "system tests." To assure integrity and objectivity, these tests are devised and conducted by a separate group rather than by the programmers. This group imagines itself the user and tries to "raise hell" with the system to make it fail.

It will fail, but only in trifling ways because the requirements were well analyzed and the system well designed to meet those requirements. Changes are made to correct the problems found, and finally a cleanly compiled system, complete with clean documentation, is ready for delivery.

Now the system is demonstrated to the customer, probably with his direct involvement, in order to win his formal acceptance. The terms of acceptance are not subjective; they were established and agreed to early in the life of the project. All that's needed now is to show that the programs meet those criteria earlier agreed to.

Once accepted, the system is delivered to the customer. If it was not possible or feasible to do acceptance testing at his installation under live conditions, there may be still another set of tests. At the conclusion of these on-site tests, the project is finished, except for any agreed follow-on work to help maintain or improve the system. Or in the case of large systems, the next versions of the system may then be built.

Now the project manager writes a history of the project's activities and makes a comparison between what was originally planned and what actually took place. He then promotes everybody and goes home to get acquainted with his family.

THE DEVELOPMENT CYCLE

The project just described need not be a fairy tale. Some projects actually *are* orderly, well managed, and successful.

The central problem with so many failed projects is loss of control because things are not kept visible enough. The requirements are often invisible, or at least obscure, because we don't take the time to make them explicit. Design and code are often invisible because, if they exist at all, they're carried around in people's heads and on private listings or scraps of paper. One of the thrusts of the newer programming technologies is to make each stage of the emerging program system visible and available for all to see.

But that's not enough. The project itself needs to be visible. It must not become an amorphous collection of people, documents, and activities. It must be divided into pieces you can get your arms around, just as a program must be divided into people-sized chunks. Make your project manageable; make it *modular*.

The way I propose that you make your project modular is by providing a framework called a *development cycle* and breaking it into a series of modules called *phases*. Dream up any number of phases you want, as long as they enable you to see and exert *control* over your project.

Chapters 2 to 7 are based on one concept of a development cycle. I've divided the cycle into six phases which make sense to me. If you need eight phases, or four, be my guest. What's important is that each phase have a very clear set of objectives and definable outputs so that all those you deal with understand your planned development cycle completely.

Define your development cycle and include its definition in your Project Plan, as I've done in Part II, Section 2.

The development cycle described in this book consists of the following phases:

Definition Phase

Design Phase

Programming Phase

System Test Phase

Acceptance Phase

Installation and Operation Phase

Each is the subject of a separate chapter in Part I. Throughout the discussion of the phases, refer to Figure I inside the front cover of the book. There the phases are depicted as vertical slices of time, implying that one phase ends and the next begins, all at some instant in time. One may argue that this is unrealistic, that in practice the phases will overlap to some degree. Although this will sometimes be true, your *aim* should be to begin a phase only when the preceding phase has been satisfactorily completed. When a phase ends, project management and the customer must decide whether the results of that phase are acceptable, and whether to start the next phase now, later, or never. Those are all possible options. In an orderly development cycle we don't build on faulty foundations.

Figure I shows a typical division of total project time among the phases. *There may be very large departures from this timing for some projects.* It's easily possible for a Definition Phase to consume a third of the total time. On a large defense project, the last two phases could take half the project's time. The parts of the development cycle most often short-changed are the front end and the rear end. On the front end, planning is often haphazard (let's get writing programs), analysis is weak (we all understand the customer's problem), and baseline design is nonexistent. On the rear end, system testing is sometimes not even included in a plan (there's no time left, and anyway, the programmers' integration test does the same job).

There is no reliable standard for time allocation; experience with similar projects is the best guide. However, most projects will not be far wrong allowing one-third of total calendar time for the Definition and Design Phases, one-third for what I have called the Programming Phase, and one-third for the rest. But even this broad rule-of-thumb is meaningless unless you understand what is included in those phases; I will describe that in succeeding chapters.

I have discussed the various topics in the book under the phases where they would normally come into the most prominence. Before considering the phases in detail, a thumbnail sketch of each should help to put things in perspective. Figure II inside the back cover of the book summarizes the phases, their functions, and important documents associated with each.

Definition Phase

During this phase, a plan for the project is written and the customer's *problem* is defined. During the problem definition activity, ideas about *solutions* will inevitably be discussed, but adoption of any specific solution is deferred until the Design Phase.

Design Phase

Now that you and the customer have agreed on what the problem is, write a design document describing an acceptable solution to the problem. Usually many solutions are feasible, but you and the customer must pick one and stick with it.

Programming Phase

You've defined the problem and blueprinted a solution; now build and test a program system according to that blueprint.

System Test Phase

After the programmers have built a product they're happy with, a separate group performs a new set of tests in as nearly a "live" environment as possible.

Acceptance Phase

The finished program system, including its documentation, is demonstrated to the customer in order to gain his formal agreement that the system satisfies the contract. Acceptance is based on meeting criteria that you and the customer agreed to earlier in the development cycle.

Installation and Operation Phase

The accepted programs are introduced into their ultimate operating environment on the customer's equipment, retested in that environment, and then put into operation.

Chapter 2

The Definition Phase

Have you ever been in a class where the teacher has begun to phrase a question, and before he can finish, a dozen eager hands are raised to offer half-baked answers? A great many program systems have been built that way. The problem has not been stated yet, but everyone is ready to program an answer! There is increasing recognition of this maniacal tendency, especially among customers who have been hurt by premature implementation and are determined next time to get a solution that matches the problem they had in mind. In the Defense Management Journal [1], a goal repeated over and over is to "Improve the operation and maintenance of [the computer system] by placing more emphasis on the requirements analysis and system design tasks. . . . Increased emphasis on the front end of . . . development should reduce the magnitude of our current software reliability problems in the future."

Sooner or later you'll have to define the problem; why not do it *first?* Problem analysis, then, is the first objective of the Definition Phase. A second objective is *project planning*, devising a scheme that will produce an acceptable solution to the problem. A third objective is writing and getting customer approval of the set of acceptance criteria which will help determine whether your product fulfills the requirements of the contract.

PROBLEM ANALYSIS

Writing a requirements document which accurately and in detail describes the customer's problem can be a very large task. In some cases it will already have been done, at least to a moderate level of detail, during proposal efforts preceding contract award. In that case, your job during the Definition Phase may be simply to fine-tune the existing documents, fill in the details, and formalize them. In other cases, the requirements will have only been sketched, and this first phase of your contract will involve plenty of analysis work. It often makes sense to contract for two separate jobs; one to define the problem and one to solve that problem.[1]

Don't assume that the problem is obvious and that everyone understands it. A friend of mine got himself in deep trouble because, after almost a year of work on his project, the problem was still changing. This was one of those in-house jobs where the work was being done under "shop order" (a sort of within-the-company contract) to another department. There never was a written definition of the job to be done. After some heated management sessions, the decision was made to salvage something and complete the job at as low a cost as possible, but nobody came out happy — neither customer, nor programming manager, nor programmers. People gag at the idea of paperwork; they are impatient to get on with the job. But this was a case, like many others, in which taking the time to define the problem would have avoided a great deal of aggravation and waste of time and money. Here the customer was part of the same company; otherwise, there might have been contract default, loss of profit, and even court action.

What, Not How

Resist the temptation to begin designing programs immediately. Concentrate first on *what* the problem is, not on *how* you are going to solve it. Certainly, while your analysts are describing the *what*, they will be thinking about and discussing design concepts. But be sure they know that their first objective is to write a document describing the problem, not the solution. Begin the document by describing the customer's problem from scratch, in nontechnical

business !
decision.

---

[1] The federal government often makes use of this principle, especially on very large contracts or when the technical problems are formidable. The government enters into an agreement with two or more contractors simultaneously and funds each to work out a problem definition and design concept. The government is then free to choose what it likes from among the various concepts submitted. A single contractor may then be chosen to go ahead with full development according to the approach chosen. The period during which the separate approaches are being worked out is usually called a Contract Definition Phase.

Some software vendors regularly do business this way. The two-stage approach limits their liability and ensures that the customer understands what he is buying.

language. Identify who the customer is, what the problem environment is, and why a computer solution is sought. Then describe the technical problem in increasing levels of detail. Be very specific about what capabilities are to be included in the system; sometimes it's helpful to point out what's *not* included. Be precise. Don't leave it to the reader to infer what's included and what is not.

Some Key Documents

We will discuss many individual documents throughout Part I and under the Documentation Plan in Part II. Right now we need to look at a few key documents that help glue the project together. The ones of interest are listed in Figure 2.1. I've chosen titles which are short and which tell you what the document is about. The word "Program" has not been tacked onto the front of each title because *all* the documents discussed in this book are about programs unless indicated otherwise. If you choose (or are forced by customer convention) to use other titles, just be sure you use them consistently.

There are three key documents shown in Figure 2.1. The first, "Problem Specification," is the document your analysts produce describing the customer's problem. It defines the *requirements* of the job to be done. The second, "Design Specification," is written during the next phase. It describes the overall solution to the problem. The third, "Coding Specification," is the detailed extension of the Design

DOCUMENT NAME	WHEN WRITTEN	WHAT IT DOES	WHO WRITES	SOME POSSIBLE FORMS
"Problem Specification"	Definition Phase	Defines the problem for which a solution is needed	Analysts	Narrative HIPO Tables Data flow diagrams Data dictionaries
"Design Specification"	Design Phase	Describes the overall solution	Designers	Narrative HIPO Tables Flow charts
"Coding Specification"	Programming Phase	Describes the detailed solution	Programmers	HIPO Pseudo code Procedure charts Code Flow charts

Figure 2.1. Key documents

Specification. It's really a *set* of documents describing the program system in detail.

On many larger projects there may be at the top of the list a broader document describing an overall problem (for example, a space-tracking system) in which the programs are only one of several major subsystems. There may be a program subsystem, a radar subsystem, a display subsystem, and so on. The document describing the overall problem is usually written by the customer or by a special system contractor. It may be called by such names as "System Specification" or "System Requirements Specification."

The document in focus during this phase, the Problem Specification, defines in quantitative terms the customer's requirements. As shown in the Documentation Plan in Part II, this specification states the requirements in four major categories:

1. *Performance*, including file capacities, timing constraints, input rates, and system loads.

2. *Functions*, or operations, to be provided by the system.

3. *Data* requirements.

4. *Human* considerations, such as minimum times for making decisions, maximum times allowable for system responses, and restrictions on program-generated displays.

Document Testing

Get used to the idea of testing your documents thoroughly, just as you test your programs. Documents such as those discussed in the preceding section, as well as user's manuals, test specifications, and so forth, are as critical to a successful project as anything you'll produce. A good way to test a document is to submit it to close scrutiny by others during a "structured walk-through" (discussed in Chapter 4). Don't simply pass a document around for comment; it's too easy for readers to be lazy and assume that the next reader will be more thorough.

There are two criteria for testing your documents. First, they must be complete and absolutely accurate. Second, they must be readable and easily understood. If sloppily organized or poorly written, it hardly matters how accurate they are because they won't be read. Your documents represent your product to the user; they're tangible, visible, while the programs are not. Making them easy to read is as important as any job on your project.

The Analysts

What kind of people do you need to do the technical analysis and write the Problem Specification? Before you select your people, consider the analyst's job:

Meet the real customer. There are usually many people who are the "customer" (see Fig. 2.2). Just as you have specialists in your organization, so does your client—and they all may make different demands on your analysts. There may be a buyer who has in mind holding down costs; a staff analyst who wants a system with a lot of fancy gadgets; a contract administrator who may know little about the technical part of the job; a user who eventually will be saddled with your system. Your analysts should not assume that the members of the customer's organization talk to each other, let alone agree about what it is you should deliver to them. If your analysts don't talk to the right people at the right time, they may not come away with a clear understanding of what this many-headed customer really expects. For example, if the analysts ignore the user until it's time to turn over a finished system, the results may be tragic. The user who

Figure 2.2. Who's the real customer?

has no part in specifying the system may be most reluctant to accept it; he may look upon it as a new gimmick being shoved down his throat. Therefore, your analysts must omit no one. They must diplomatically find out who controls what, who has the real power, and who will eventually use the product.

Pick the customer's brains. The analysts must be skilled at finding out what the customer *really* wants because it may be different from what was implied in a loosely worded contract. They need to read both what they're given and what's between the lines. They need to interview people and try to understand what's really being said. They must listen hard, rephrase what the customer has said, feed it back to him and ask: Is this what you mean?

Write it down. The analysts can write the Problem Specification in an infinite number of ways. Some of those ways will be easy for designers to implement, some difficult, some impossible. An analysis team lacking programming experience can kill you. (By the way, so can a team with *only* programming experience.) The analysts must state the problem in clear and precise language that is acceptable to both the customer and your designers. Keep it simple. Don't tolerate any of those programming people whom Robert Townsend [2] calls "complicators, not simplifiers."

Get it approved — gradually. As they write sections of the Problem Specification, the analysts should get tentative customer approval of what they have written. Don't show the customer your finished document all at once, for if he doesn't like it, you're in bad shape. Let him in on what you're doing as you go along. No surprises, please.

Obviously, then, the analyst should represent many disciplines: programmer, salesman, engineer, psychologist, writer. You won't often find all the attributes you need in one person, but you can build a group that collectively has all the right credentials. Don't rely on titles when you select your people. There are many people around called "analysts" because they don't neatly fit any other category.

PROJECT PLANNING

Too many programming projects are treated like mystery novels. You're left hanging by your fingernails down to the last climactic moment when it's suddenly clear which manager was the villain. One programming manager I know of, on a year-long job, reported every-thing "on-schedule" until a month before the deadline. Then he informed the customer that he would be a month late. When the new target date arrived, he nervously offered still another date, two months later. And when that time arrived, his former manager took over as programming manager and with a great burst of energy finished the job nine months later. A year late on a one-year job. How come?

Over the years I've had the opportunity to listen to the plaints of hundreds of managers and programmers from many different com-panies and government agencies. I've seen surveys taken in an attempt to ferret out problem areas. And of course I've pondered the prob-lems I've personally encountered. A list of the problems which most often boil to the surface looks something like this:

- Poor planning

- Ill-defined contract

- Poor planning

- Unstable problem definition

- Poor planning

- Inexperienced management

- Poor planning

- Political pressures

- Poor planning

- Ineffective change control

- Poor planning

- Unrealistic deadlines

- Poor planning

The list could be several pages long and two items would remain conspicuous, one by its presence, another by its absence. Ever present is *poor planning*. Sometimes that means failure to consider the job from all angles, and sometimes it means there is essentially no plan at all. Absent from the list is *technical difficulty*. That's not to say that many jobs aren't technically tough, but there are few that are beyond the "state-of-the-art." In fact, if you agree to do a job that *is* beyond the state-of-the-art, a job that requires some technical breakthrough, *that's* poor planning. (An obvious exception is a project whose objective is some sort of basic research.)

The System

The thing we're planning to build is called a *system*. Let's define what that is. *A system is a structured combination of interacting parts satisfying a set of objectives.* That's pretty starchy, but maybe it will make better sense after citing a few examples and examining some characteristics of systems.

There are examples of systems everywhere you look: the solar system; a power distribution system; the human body; the digestive system; a corporation; a pencil sharpener; a computer system. They all satisfy the definition.

Every system is really a subset of some other system. This book will frequently mention a programming "system," but of course the programming system is really a *sub*system of a data-processing system, which in turn may be a *sub*system of a weapon system, which is a *sub*system of a defense system, and on and on it goes.

Characteristics of a System

Books have been written on this subject alone. We'll consider here only a few of the characteristics that make it difficult to build a system.

Interactions. By definition, a system contains parts which must interact with each other. The parts, in the case of programming systems, may be supervisor programs, application programs, service programs, hardware, human operators, human users, and so on. Controlling the interactions among the parts becomes a major task as the system grows in size and complexity.

Figure 2.3 illustrates how the number of *potential* interactions (I) within a system grows as the number of elements (E) in the system grows. The management energy required to control, minimize,

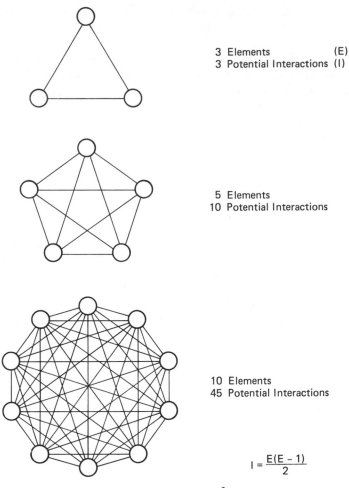

3 Elements   (E)
3 Potential Interactions (I)

5 Elements
10 Potential Interactions

10 Elements
45 Potential Interactions

$$I = \frac{E(E - 1)}{2}$$

Figure 2.3. Interactions[2]

and simplify the interactions within the system is significant. Interactions account for much of the difference between managing the development of a small program having a single function and managing the development of an operating system or a payroll system. Interactions can be controlled if we first recognize that they exist. Later chapters will discuss such concepts as modularity, interface definition, and project organization, which can help minimize the

[2] Reprinted by permission from *Programming Project Management Guide*, International Business Machines Corporation, 1970.

effects of interactions. Realize, though, that interactions are always there and must be dealt with consciously, not ignored.

Change. Given any job that spans more than a couple of weeks of time, you can be sure that change will occur. Examples of the kinds of changes are as follows:

- *Requirements changes:* The problem definition your analysts labor over at the beginning of the job seldom stands still. The larger the job, the more likely there will be shifts in the requirements.

- *Design changes:* One of the main items we'll look at in the next chapter is a baseline design, intended as the foundation for your programming effort. But, as any homeowner knows, foundations shift, crack, and have to be patched. A program system is no different. Treat your baseline design as a good start, but expect it to be changed.

- *Technological changes:* The huge government-sponsored programming jobs (e.g., anti-ballistic missile systems, military command and control systems) are particularly vulnerable to technological change for two reasons. First, they span such long periods of time that new engineering and scientific developments (for example, in weaponry and data-processing equipment) are inevitable. Second, the very nature of these projects is that they push the state-of-the-art and are often directly *responsible* for technological innovation.

- *Social changes:* Many projects are the unwitting victims of changes in the way a large segment of society behaves. For example, programs to handle payroll checks are constantly bombarded with changes because the tax laws change or because people make new demands on the system by having more and more personal deductions made.

- *People changes:* People leave, die, get sick, change jobs. When you lose a key person from your own staff or when an important member of the customer's organization disappears, you have a potential problem.

- *Corrections:* People make errors. They always have and they always will. The errors may be major or minor, technical or administrative, outrageous or subtle, but they are errors none-theless, and they must be fixed.

What's important about change is that it be *controlled*, not eliminated. If there is a change in the Problem Specification, so be it, but estimate the impact of the change on project costs and delivery dates. If the customer still wants the change, negotiate a contract modification, issue a formal change notice, and get on with the job.

Whenever there is a question of change, one thing is of paramount importance: there can be no resolution of questions such as the cost of a change if you and your customer cannot even agree that what is being discussed *is* a change. You say: "This change, Mr. Customer, will cost ten extra man-months and a two-month slip in the delivery date." He says: "What change? This is only something I expected to get for my money in the first place. Quit gouging me." So you frantically thumb through your Problem Specification, assuming you have one at all, and each of you tries to find a paragraph, statement, clause, or comma to back up your position.

What I've described is an exercise repeated every day, all too often ending in deadlock. That's why throughout this book I emphasize establishing accurate and meaningful baseline documents.

The support system. It's worth noting that there are really two systems of concern to you. One, of course, is the system you are trying to build — your product. The second, not always recognized, is the collection of people, tools, and procedures needed to do the building. The elements of the support system are subject to the same stresses (for example, interactions and change) as the systems being built. The manager has to consider both.

Planning Tools

Maybe someday a genius will devise a planning language that will do for the planner what FORTRAN or PL/1 does for the programmer. Then you'll be able to code some planning statements, run them through a computer, and presto! — out comes a plan. Until that happens, however, we'll all have to be content with more mundane methods.

Project plan outline. The toughest part of any writing job is getting started. Once you've decided on a format and a detailed outline, things flow more easily. The Project Plan outlined in Part II should serve to get you going quickly. Use it as a starter, modify it to suit your situation, and you're on the way.

Starting with the outline described in Part II will pay off in several ways. First, you won't waste time trying to decide how to break up the planning job. Second, this outline has built-in credibility because it has been contributed to by many experienced programming managers. Third, having *any* outline to use as a starter helps reduce the number of rewrites. I've witnessed many planning exercises (such as writing proposals) in which writing assignments were loosely made according to a very sketchy outline or with no outline at all. Hundreds of man-hours later someone finally firms up an outline and a massive rewriting ensues — not to change technical content, but simply to make all the sections of the document fit together. These early days in planning or proposal writing are hectic enough; why make things worse by guaranteeing false starts?

Bar charts. Almost everyone is familiar with bar charts (also called Gantt charts) in one form or another. They are simple to construct and can be useful in depicting the scheduling or expenditure of resources versus time.

A simple example of a bar chart is shown in Figure 2.4 which tells at a glance who is assigned to which tasks. The tasks can be as big or as small as you wish; what's important is that their size provide you the control you need. As a project manager, you will probably want a chart that shows the large tasks, but your first-level managers (those who directly supervise the programmers) will need charts showing the small tasks. For example, if your project is to write a system involving some real-time message processing, *you* may want a chart showing such tasks as "input-message error processing," "input-message error recognition," "input-message error correction," and "input-message routing." These tasks may be of several months' duration. Since the first-level manager, however, could scarely exercise any control against a chart that broad, *he* needs to break each task into smaller pieces so that trouble can be spotted early. Theoretically, his maximum exposure is equal to the longest-duration task.

How finely you break down your tasks depends on the complexity of that part of the job and the experience and competence of the programmers. You might subdivide a given task into three one-week pieces for one programmer, but for another you might assign that same task in one two-week chunk. As a general guideline, however, the minimum time any task should be scheduled for is a week; a

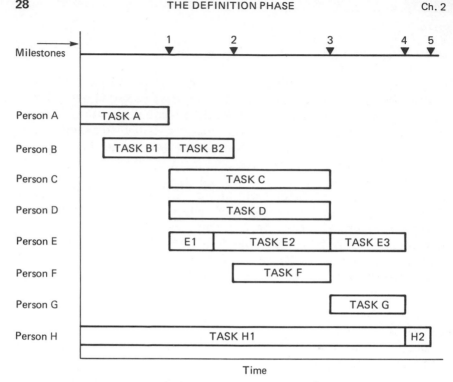

Time

Figure 2.4. Simple bar chart[3]

more reasonable time in most cases would be two weeks. If you try to subdivide tasks any finer, your programmers will spend disproportionate amounts of time in progress reporting rather than in progress, and your first-level managers will become bookkeepers because they'll be preoccupied with logging and keeping track of all those little tasks. (I remember one project in which the reporting got to be *daily*. It wasn't very long before the only progress reported was completion of the previous day's report.)

The maximum time most tasks should be scheduled for is about a month—and again, two weeks would be more comfortable. The point is that if a task is in trouble, you've got to know it soon enough to take remedial action. It's not very helpful to report the day before the project deadline that you're two months late.

Bar charts may be used in many different ways. Figure 2.4 shows

[3] Reprinted by permission from *Programming Project Management Guide,* International Business Machines Corporation, 1970.

people, tasks, and time. Other charts might simply show tasks versus time, computer-time requirements versus time, or anything versus anything, as long as they help you in planning and controlling. The tasks shown on a chart should be listed and defined on a separate sheet. Every task must require the delivery of a clearly defined product, such as a program module or a document.

Milestone charts. Webster defines a milestone as a "significant point in development." When you define milestones for your project, don't forget that word *significant*. Don't necessarily make the end of each task a milestone. Instead, pick out those points in your schedules at which something truly significant should have been completed and at which some decision is to be made, for example, continue, replan, get more resources. Further, base each milestone on something *measurable;* otherwise, you won't know when you get there. Here are some examples of *poor* milestones:

- "Testing 50% complete." Even if "50% complete" means something to you, chances are it will mean something different to someone else. It's a poor milestone because there is no sure way of knowing when you get there—it's not *measurable*. Even if based on the number of tests to be run, it's fuzzy because tests vary so much in complexity that one "half" may take a week to run and the other "half" may take three months.

- "Coding 50% complete." The same objections apply here. Who knows that the coding is 50% complete? Does this mean 50% of the anticipated number of lines of code? Or 50% of the modules are coded? Maybe 50% of the lines are coded, but they're the "easy" 50%, with the crunchers yet to come. Again, the number is deceptive because it means different things to different people.

- "Module X keypunched." Who cares? This is significant to the individual programmer, but it means very little to you in managing the overall project unless, perhaps, module X is already a year late or keypunch service has been your curse in the past.

Here are a few examples of *good* milestones for the *first-level manager.*

- "Detailed design on module X approved." That's important even though that design may later be changed. It means that the program module is laid out on paper and is ready for coding.

- "Module X coded." This is helpful but not as helpful as some other milestones because the code may change radically as testing goes on.

- "Module testing of module X completed." This means that the programmer has tested his individual module of code to his satisfaction and it's ready for integration with other tested modules. It's a good milestone because the programmer at this point actually submits his physical program for the next level of testing. It also means, as will be explained later, that the descriptive documentation for that module is completed in draft form, and this is something else that is measurable — something you can actually hold in your hands and see.

- "Specification Y drafted." Again, the document is either physically done or it isn't. The manager can take a quick look at it and decide whether or not it's in good enough shape to be considered done, and hence whether or not the milestone has been met.

Figure 2.5 offers the *project manager* a list of basic milestones for each development phase. Modify the list to suit you. Some of the items listed will make better sense after you have read later chapters.

How many milestones should you have? As usual, there is no magic number, but consider these guidelines:

- Each manager should have his own set of milestones for the work to be done by the people reporting to him. This means that the first-level manager has milestones for the programmers' work, the programming manager has milestones for the first-level managers' work, and so on. However, one manager's milestones are not simply the sum of all those used by the managers who report to him. Each manager at each higher level must concentrate his energy on broader problems; that, after all, is what hierarchical organizations are all about.

- Don't define the end of every task as a milestone. Allow some flexibility. For example, if a series of four tasks leads to a

MILESTONE	WHEN
• Problem specification written • Accepted by customer • Draft project plan completed • Preliminary program acceptance test specification written • Accepted by customer	End of definition phase
• Preliminary design specification written • Accepted by customer	Middle of design phase
• Design specification completed • Accepted by customer • First distribution of programmer's handbook • Design phase review completed • Program integration test specification completed	End of design phase
• Program system test specification completed • Final program acceptance test specification and site test specification written • Approved by customer • All program documentation completed in clean draft form	End of programming phase
• System test completed	End of system test phase
• Acceptance agreement signed • Customer training completed	End of acceptance phase
• Program documentation corrected and delivered • System operational • Project history completed	End of installation and operation phase

Figure 2.5. Project milestones

milestone, this allows those responsible for the four tasks to do some juggling in order to meet the milestone.

• Milestones should be considered important enough that the people on the project will put out some extra effort in order to meet a milestone that seems to be in jeopardy. This means that you should have few enough that you don't have a weekly milestone crisis. After three or four of these crises, your people will begin to yawn when you scream for help. (Coincidentally, just after I wrote this section I chatted with a programmer down the hall. It was Saturday, and I was working on the book while the programmer was working on what he considered an unnecessary fire call. He complained that there seemed to be one of these crises every week. It was obvious to me that if a real schedule crisis should arise, this man would not get excited, because as far as he was concerned, his manager cried "wolf" too often.)

• The milestones used by your first-level managers should ordinarily be spaced *at least* two weeks apart; for the next higher level, at least three weeks apart; next, four weeks, and so on.

Activity networks. Bar charts are useful, but they have one significant weakness: they don't adequately show *interdependencies* among tasks or among people. To show these interdependencies an activity network chart is needed.

Figure 2.6 is an example of a very simple activity network for the job laid out in Figure 2.4. The circles represent events; the lines show activities that are required to get from one event to the next. The estimated units of time for each activity, or task, are shown in parentheses. The lines feeding an event circle from the left represent activities that must be finished before that event can occur. For example, to arrive at event 4 activities H1, E3, and G must be completed.

In this example the job is so simple that all interdependencies can be easily visualized. The times add up nicely, there is no problem, and the network chart tells us nothing that we didn't already know from the bar chart. Suppose, however, that task E1 (Figure 2.4) cannot really begin until B2 is finished. Now you have a problem, and something's got to give. Either B2 must be started earlier (which may be impossible), E1, E2, E3 cannot be scheduled serially, the project end date must slip, or some other rearrangement must be made. These interdependencies come to light as you construct an activity chart, because you must constantly satisfy the question: What must be done before I begin the next task? This exercise is particularly useful on larger projects when it's difficult to visualize all the activities going on.

Normally, when a network chart is finished, there will be a path from beginning to end over which the total time required will be greater than for any other path. This route is called the *critical*

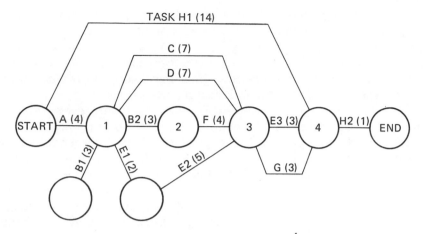

Figure 2.6. Simple activity network[4]

path. It demands extra monitoring and management attention, for if it slips, the end date slips.

The activity network is most valuable during the design and integration test activities when management attention is directed toward the problems of fitting things together. It is less useful during the middle time when individual program modules are being written and tested, because then the focus is on individual pieces of the system more than on their interactions. Since the usefulness of these charts falls off after design is completed, they are often abandoned at that time. This may explain why PERT[5] has had only spotty success in programming. The effort required to keep PERT activity networks updated as the project progresses is costly and it diverts managers from supervising individual tasks. It is not uncommon for a network to deteriorate during the Programming Phase. If it falls behind, abandon it. Don't blindly update it if it's no longer useful.

The activity network could be drawn according to a time scale, with the spacing between event circles representing calendar time. These charts require a lot of work and tend to cover walls, which is all right if you don't like your walls. I suggest that bar charts be used to show calendar schedules and that activity networks be limited to showing interdependencies.

[4] Reprinted by permission from *Programming Project Management Guide*, International Business Machines Corporation, 1970.

[5] PERT, Program Evaluation and Review Technique, is a formalized, usually computerized implementation of the activity network idea. There are several basic forms and many specific versions of PERT networks. Since the literature abounds with books and articles on the subject, they will not be discussed here.

Estimating guidelines. Estimating the size of the job to be done is probably one of the toughest tasks a manager faces. Nobody has succeeded in coming up with a cookbook to make the estimating process mechanical or automatic, but there are some steps you can take to approach the problem with a reasonable degree of sanity. First, however, let's understand what an estimate is.

An estimate is *your judgment* of what a job will cost in terms of man-years, calendar time, machine-hours, and other resources. It is a statement of how you plan to expend resources in order to get the job done. When translated into money and calendar time, and adopted for your project, the estimate is called a *budget.*

Your Project Plan must *evolve* and change whenever conditions change. The same applies to your estimate or budget: If changes requiring more resources take place, you must reestimate and change the budget. Estimates will always be imperfect and will need refining as the project rolls along. Ideally, your contract should be written to allow for estimating each new phase at the end of the preceding one.

Here is one way to approach the estimating process. Although this section logically is placed here under the general heading of "Planning Tools," it will be more meaningful if you review it once you have read the rest of the book.

STEP 1. Design the program system. I can hear you muttering, "What does he mean, *design the system?* That's part of the job I'm trying to estimate!" The truth is that you *can* design your system to some level of detail. The design might be only four pages of charts requiring a day's effort but that's a whole lot better than nothing. You *must* take the time to consider the magnitude of the problem you're estimating. It's patently impossible to estimate the cost of building something completely undefined. In fact, *the key to successful estimating is understanding the problem.*

The design you develop for your first estimating exercise should be carried to a level at which you have a feel for all the major technical problems that you will face. If you can take the time to design the program system in detail, that's great. More likely, however, your design (at least for *initial* estimates) will be at a much broader level. No matter how broad, you'll still have a better basis for an estimate than if you were to resort to the random number method.

STEP 2. Estimate the total size of the program system to be delivered. By size I mean the number of final, deliverable lines of code there will be, including code that defines data files as well as code that defines executable machine instructions. Get at this number by estimating the size of each module in your design and then adding them together. The more detailed your design the more accurate this total estimate is likely to be. If you plan to code in more than one language (for example, assembler language and FORTRAN), find a separate total for each. If you are modifying an existing system, estimate the lines of new code that you will write.

STEP 3. Estimate the *programming* manpower (see Fig. 2.7a) required to produce the number of lines of code that you have just derived. Each organization has its own rules of thumb regarding numbers of finished instructions per man-day or man-month. There is no published set of these numbers in the programming community better than the informal rules that you have in your own organization. If you use someone else's numbers, question them. For example, if someone says that a good rule of thumb is five instructions per man-day, you need to know several things about that number: Does it cover only the programmer's time? Does it include problem analysis and baseline design? Does it include module test? Integration test? System test? Acceptance test? Documentation? Management time? Support personnel? What language is used?

STEP 4. Estimate the *support* manpower requirements suggested in Figure 2.7a. Not all the items listed in this and other checklists are necessarily applicable to *your* job. In later discussions of organization I'll offer some typical numbers of support personnel, but here again your own experience may be worth far more than any numbers you get from a book.

STEP 5. Estimate equipment costs. Figure 2.7b is intended to remind you of the various categories of equipment and users you might need to consider for your job. Again, later chapters will have more to say on testing and machine time.

STEP 6. Estimate the items in Figure 2.7c that apply to you.

STEP 7. Now that you've sized everything in a sort of bare-bones way, go back and add whatever contingencies are appropriate for your organization. For example, you may have shown a requirement for 500 man-months of programmers' time, but programmers get sick, take vacations, quit, get fired, go on military duty, and so on. These items may easily reduce the average person's effectiveness on your job by 20%. If you assume 100% use of anybody's time, you'll be in trouble right off the bat. Decide what the numbers should be for your organization and use them to modify your estimates (either manpower or calendar time, or both). *Write down* all your contingency factors so that others looking at your estimate will know what you did.

STEP 8. Consider such weighting facors as those suggested in Figure 2.8. Check off each item that you think applies to your job. For each item checked, ask whether or not you have already taken it into account in your estimate. If not, decide whether each is of sufficient value to cause you to increase your estimate. In each case there are various parts of your estimate that may be affected, but you can reasonably limit yourself to the three largest items: manpower, computer time, and calendar time.

The list is rigged so that any item checked would normally suggest an *increase* in your estimates. For any item *not* checked, it may mean that your estimate should be left alone, as far as that point is concerned, or it may suggest that negative weighting is in order — that is, you might *decrease* your original estimate. But go easy — estimates in this business are very seldom too high.

STEP 9. Now convert everything to money, by applying average salary rates, machine time rates, etc. for your organization. If pricing

---

```
          POTENTIAL COST ITEMS

[ ]  Programming manpower
     [ ]  Programmers
     [ ]  First–level programming managers
     [ ]  Programmer librarians
[ ]  Support manpower
     [ ]  Analysts
     [ ]  Designers
     [ ]  Testers
     [ ]  Managers
     [ ]  Engineers
     [ ]  Secretaries
     [ ]  Typists
     [ ]  Instructors
     [ ]  Computer operators
     [ ]  Keypunch operators
     [ ]  Administrative assistants
     [ ]  Financial assistants
     [ ]  General librarians
     [ ]  Technical writers
     [ ]  Clerical assistants
     [ ]  Couriers
     [ ]  Consultants
```

Figure 2.7. (*a*) Estimating checklist: Manpower

```
┌─────────────────────────────────────────────────┐
│              POTENTIAL COST ITEMS               │
├─────────────────────────────────────────────────┤
│  [ ]  Computer time                             │
│       [ ]  Users                                │
│            [ ]  Operational programmers         │
│            [ ]  Support programmers             │
│            [ ]  Analysts and designers          │
│            [ ]  Management                       │
│            [ ]  Maintenance people              │
│       [ ]  Uses                                 │
│            [ ]  Assembly and compilation        │
│            [ ]  Module  test                    │
│            [ ]  Integration test                │
│            [ ]  System test                     │
│            [ ]  Acceptance test                 │
│            [ ]  Site test                       │
│            [ ]  Installation of support programs│
│            [ ]  Simulation                      │
│            [ ]  Report generation               │
│            [ ]  PERT                            │
│            [ ]  Program maintenance             │
│            [ ]  Hardware maintenance            │
│            [ ]  Contingency reserve             │
│       [ ]  Configurations                       │
│            [ ]  CPU's                           │
│            [ ]  Core storage sizes              │
│            [ ]  I/O devices                     │
│  [ ]  Keypunch time                             │
│       [ ]  Users                                │
│            [ ]  Programmers                      │
│            [ ]  Analysts and designers          │
│            [ ]  Management                       │
│            [ ]  Testers                         │
│       [ ]  Uses                                 │
│            [ ]  Programs                         │
│            [ ]  Data base                       │
│            [ ]  Test data                       │
│            [ ]  Report data                     │
│            [ ]  Spares for programmer use       │
│  [ ]  Other equipment costs                     │
│       [ ]  Communications                       │
│       [ ]  Programming terminals                │
│       [ ]  Special changes to standard equipment│
│       [ ]  Automated documentation systems      │
│       [ ]  Document reproduction equipment      │
│       [ ]  Microimage readers                   │
└─────────────────────────────────────────────────┘
```

Figure 2.7. (*b*) Estimating checklist: Equipment

```
┌─────────────────────────────────────────────────────┐
│                POTENTIAL COST ITEMS                  │
├─────────────────────────────────────────────────────┤
│ [ ]  Physical facilities                            │
│        [ ]  General (office space, furniture, etc.) │
│        [ ]  Special for your project                │
│               [ ]  Document storage                 │
│               [ ]  Card storage                     │
│               [ ]  Tape storage                     │
│               [ ]  Disk storage                     │
│               [ ]  Classified storage               │
│               [ ]  Program pick-up and drop areas   │
│               [ ]  Reproduction equipment area      │
│ [ ]  Supplies                                       │
│        [ ]  General (paper, pencils, etc.)          │
│        [ ]  Special for your project                │
│               [ ]  Computer printer paper           │
│               [ ]  Cards                            │
│               [ ]  Paper tape                       │
│               [ ]  Magnetic tapes                   │
│               [ ]  Diskettes                        │
│               [ ]  Carrying cases                   │
│               [ ]  Film                             │
│ [ ]  Relocations                                    │
│        [ ]  Moving people                           │
│        [ ]  Moving equipment and facilities         │
│ [ ]  Trips                                          │
│        [ ]  Reasons                                 │
│               [ ]  For computer time                │
│               [ ]  Visit customer                   │
│               [ ]  Visit other contractors          │
│               [ ]  Attend professional meetings, symposiums │
│        [ ]  Number of trips                         │
│        [ ]  Number of people per trip               │
│        [ ]  Duration of trips                       │
│ [ ]  Special publication costs (work done by publications │
│        organization outside your project)           │
│ [ ]  Other                                          │
│        [ ]  Shuttle service to computers            │
│               [ ]  Cars                             │
│               [ ]  Drivers                          │
│        [ ]  Leased program systems                  │
│        [ ]  Purchased program systems               │
│        [ ]  Shift premiums                          │
│        [ ]  Overtime payments                       │
│        [ ]  Per diem payments                       │
│        [ ]  Special training aids                   │
└─────────────────────────────────────────────────────┘
```

Figure 2.7. (c) Estimating checklist: Miscellaneous.

specialists handle this task for you, be sure that they understand what you have included and be sure you know what they may add on. For example, they may normally add the contingencies mentioned in Step 7.

STEP 10. The estimate you have so far is the *base cost* for the job, sometimes called *factory cost* or *direct cost.* Now, add your profit, your overhead expense, and any fees not already included. This is the completed cost estimate for the job. But you're not done yet.

STEP 11. Write down the *assumptions* on which your estimate is based. Do not pass your estimate on to *anyone* without giving him the assumptions. Nail the estimate and the assumptions together if you have to. You may have made some assumptions that your boss can't live with or that are impossible to meet. Your estimate may be totally useless if it's based on a bad assumption. Don't include in very fine print an assumption that you *know* is impossible to meet in order to save your hide if the project gets in trouble later on. Besides being childish and unethical, it won't work.

STEP 12. As the job progresses through the development cycle, reestimate all or portions of the job as you get better and better inputs. A major point for reestimating is at the end of the Design Phase. At that time you should have not only a complete system design as the basis for your estimate but a solid Project Plan as well. The process of writing the Project Plan will have greatly sharpened your awareness of all cost items you're likely to face.

Your new estimate may show a need for simply rejuggling your total resources (for example, using fewer people but more machine time); this is usually within a project manager's purview. If, however, the new estimate shows a need for *additional* resources, you may have a problem. Whether or not you can get the additional resources depends on the kind of contract you have and on the understanding and credibility existing between you and your customer. In many cases you can demonstrate that there has been a change in the work scope, and the customer will amend the contract to reflect the changes. Frequently an agreement can be reached in which the program requirements will be pared to fit the resources the customer can offer. Probably just as frequently you will end up doing more work than you are paid for—a fact that underscores our inability to estimate accurately enough the first time around.

FACTORS WHICH MAY INCREASE YOUR ESTIMATE
[ ]   Vague job requirements
[ ]   Innovation required
[ ]   System will have more than one user
[ ]   System will be installed at more than one location
[ ]   System is real–time
[ ]   System is weapons control
[ ]   Interfaces with other systems are ill–defined or complex
[ ]   Your programs are to interface with other programs
[ ]   You are to modify someone else's programs
[ ]   Your analysts have not worked on a similar application
[ ]   Your designers have not worked on a similar application
[ ]   Your programmers have not worked on a similar application
[ ]   Your managers have not worked on a similar application
[ ]   The system is larger than those you have usually worked on
[ ]   You must share computer time with other projects
[ ]   You do not have complete control of computer or keypunch resources
[ ]   Customer has control of computer or keypunch resources
[ ]   You are obliged to adhere to government Configuration Management standards and procedures
[ ]   Your background is not in programming
[ ]   Customer will supply data base
[ ]   Customer will supply test data
[ ]   Data base is complex or not yet defined
[ ]   Data base is classified for security reasons
[ ]   Your programmers must be trained in a new coding language
[ ]   Your programmers must be trained on a new computer
[ ]   You cannot make use of a proven, existing operating system or input-output package
[ ]   You must provide your own support programs
[ ]   You must test on a computer not identical to the eventual operational computer
[ ]   Your effort is split among several locations
[ ]   You have a high percentage of new or junior programmers
[ ]   Computer storage is severely limited
[ ]   Input-output is limited in terms of speed, channels, or storage capacity

Figure 2.8. Weighting factors [4]

[ ]   Computer turnaround time is greater than 2 hours

[ ]   Computer turnaround time is unpredictable

[ ]   Your designers are not expert programmers

[ ]   Your confidence in personnel continuity is low

[ ]   You have little or no choice of personnel who work for you

[ ]   The customer must sign off on your design

[ ]   Other agencies must sign off on your design

[ ]   Customer is inexperienced in data processing

[ ]   Customer is experienced in data processing

[ ]   You must work on customer premises (cuts down on facility costs, but customer can bug you more easily)

[ ]   You expect much change during development, either in system requirements or in design constraints or in customer personnel

[ ]   The system has a large number of functions

[ ]   The working environment promises many interruptions

Figure 2.8. (Continued)

Project histories. Probably one of the most miserable failures in the data processing business is that of keeping accurate records of estimates versus actual expenditures. The difficulty in doing this industrywide is that everyone operates differently and it's tough to agree on any standard way of keeping records. But there is no reason why a given organization cannot and should not compile such data, perhaps with the help of an automated control system. I urge you to keep histories for your projects and then *use* them in planning succeeding jobs. It's worth your taking the time to define what records should be kept as part of a history, and it's worth designating someone sharp as a historian. In Part II, under Documentation Plan, I suggest an outline for a Project History. Use it, or devise one of your own, but avoid simply gathering a lot of charts and documents, slapping a cover on them, and labelling the whole mess "Project History." Such piles of paper are useless.

In order for a set of project history data to be helpful on your next job, you must be able to relate the two jobs. I suggest you adopt a development cycle, such as described in this book, and stick to it from one project to the next. Then when you list manpower or computer time costs for items such as "module test," "integration test," and "system test," those terms will mean the same thing on the new job you're estimating as they did on the previous jobs for which you have kept histories.

The Project Plan

The Project Plan is the subject of Part II and is outlined there in detail. In addition, various elements of the plan are discussed at appropriate places in the following chapters. At this point it's sufficient to orient ourselves by taking a brief look at the plan.

Characteristics of a good plan. A plan is a roadmap showing how to get from here to there. Like a roadmap, it indicates alternate routes, landmarks, and distances. Here are some of the things a good plan is and is not:

- It's *in writing*, not in the manager's head.

- It describes *what* the job is, *how* it will be attacked, and the *resources* required to do it.

- It's written with care so that it's *readable*, not just an accumulation of papers whose relation to one another is obscure. Pay particular attention to plan continuity. If you begin with the model plan outlined in this book, you'll have a good start toward continuity.

- It allows for *contingencies:* it states actions to be taken in case something does not go as planned. There are two types of contingency planning to consider. The first involves specific, identifiable problems which may arise (for example, if a planned computer is not available on the date specified, where will test time be obtained, and at what added cost in time and money?). The second is tougher: what actions will be taken in case unforeseen problems develop? Obviously, specific answers cannot be supplied because specific problems cannot be stated. But the manager can prepare for such events by being realistic in planning resources. Always assume people will get sick, leave the company, get pregnant, misunderstand a specification, make mistakes. Always assume machines will break down. Always assume misunderstandings with the customer. Plan the best you can to make eveything work perfectly, but understand that will never happen. Allow extra resources to cover the unplanned obstacles.

- It's *modular*. If books were not written in parts, chapters, and paragraphs, reading them would be exhausting. The same applies to any piece of writing, including a plan. The document must be logically subdivided so that there is a reasonable flow from one section to the next, but so that each section still retains its identity and is useful on a stand-alone basis.

- It's *brief* enough that it won't turn people off. Mounds of paper simply will not be read. The plan could be as small as one page for each section. More likely, it will require, for our hypothetical project, a notebook of perhaps forty or fifty pages. That's not too much to ask each project member to read. After having read it once, most people will need only refer to specific sections of the plan from time to time. How big your plan grows depends in part on how much tutorial filler you include. You need enough discussion to define terms and to guide the reader through the plan, but remember that too much bulk in your plan will cause it to go unread and unused.

- It has an *index*. It only takes a short time to construct a decent alphabetical index, and its inclusion will greatly enhance the usefulness of the document.

Writing the project plan. So far I've considered planning as though it never begins until you have a signed contract and your project is under way. In practice, however, this is rarely the case. Your project's Definition Phase will usually have been preceded by any number of planning activities: your own studies and proposal efforts; customer-funded studies; prior, related contracts; discussions between you and your prospective customer. Thus, your planning activity may be considered only one step in an evolutionary process, and this evolution does not end when your Definition Phase ends. No matter how good a plan you devise, it will change throughout the life of your project. Even so, the plan you produce during the Definition Phase should be as complete and self-contained as you can make it *at that time*.

The people who contribute to your Project Plan should include analysts, programmers, and managers, all of whom are to have continuing responsibility on the project. The user, too, must either participate or at least provide input. Leave out any one of them and the plan will probably be unreal. One individual arbitrates and has the final say in areas of dispute: that's you. If you go off politicking and tell your planning group to dream up a plan for you to rubber-stamp, you're wasting everybody's time. If you don't really believe in planning and don't intend to use the plan to help guide you during the project, admit it. You're a dynamic manager and you're going to "wing it." Good luck.

The planning team should be as small as possible in order to reduce interactions and produce a plan that hangs together. The plan should not read as if it were written by a dozen different people who never talk to one another.

To get on with the planning job, first decide on a rough outline. I suggest that you simply lift the model plan outline in Part II of this book and then spend a couple of hours adapting it to suit your own ideas. Next, decide how much calendar time you can afford to spend in the planning activity. (We'll discuss this later.)

Now consider all the individuals you have available to do the planning — their talents, strengths, weaknesses — and assign them appropriate pieces of the plan along with a schedule of dates when you expect to see completed drafts. The model plan presented in this book is divided into sections, or subplans, which provide a handy basis for doling out the work. For this hypothetical forty-person project, four planners, besides yourself, are probably sufficient.

When you're ready to hand out planning assignments, have a kickoff meeting including everyone working for or with you on this project. With everyone (both planners and analysts) together in the same room at the same time, define and discuss the project's objectives. Then discuss any constraints under which the project must operate, such as fixed deadlines, customer-imposed milestones, funding, and work location.

Having set the stage, now assign sections of the Project Plan to individuals. If you have already done this before the meeting, be sure now that everyone knows not only *his* assignment, but the assignments of the other project members. Write down names, assignments, and dates when material is due to you, and give everyone present a copy of the list.

Follow up the kickoff meeting with periodic status meetings in which planners (and analysts) can describe their progress and in which you can assess overall status relative to approaching target dates.

The Definition Phase and the Design Phase together should be allotted from about one-fourth to one-half of the total contract time. Planning is a major activity during both those phases. You will find it all too easy to slight your planning activity because you're anxious to get on with the programming. But if you don't take the time to plan well, you'll more than pay for it in later phases when things fall apart. Testing will falter, schedules will be missed, budgets will be overrun, and quite likely the quality of your product will suffer. Maybe *you* don't mind the chaos of a poorly planned project, but how about your people? Maybe they would rather not work eighty-hour weeks. If they are deprived of a pleasant, broadening work experience, or if their private lives are severely impacted because of poor project planning, the management of the job is a failure.

A project plan outline. I tried many different structures before settling on the outline presented here and in Part II. I think you'll find it helpful, but by all means modify it to suit your needs, even your temperament. After all, you have to live with it.

The Project Plan is divided into the following sections, which are summarized in succeeding paragraphs:

Overview

Phase Plan

Organization Plan

Test Plan

Change Control Plan

Documentation Plan

Training Plan

Review and Reporting Plan

Installation and Operation Plan

Resources and Deliverables Plan

Index

Overview. This section of the plan has three purposes: First, it assumes that the reader knows nothing about the project and it introduces him to the job and to the customer. Second, it describes the general organization of the plan. Third, it summarizes the entire plan by giving a capsule description of the detailed plan elements that follow the Overview.

Phase Plan. The objective of this section is to define the development cycle for your project. The Phase Plan serves as a foundation for subsequent plan elements.

If you choose to adopt a development cycle the same as the one presented in this book, then your Phase Plan will amount to a condensation of Part I. There should, however, be one significant difference, aside from sheer volume: Your Phase Plan should end with a chart similar to Figure I (inside the front cover of the book), but with *dates included.*

The Phase Plan provides you with a base, a point of reference. For example, when you and your people talk about the System Test Phase, *you should all be talking about the same thing.* I have rarely seen that happen on a project, and that's a crime. It leads to much confusion and misunderstanding that could easily be avoided.

Organization Plan. This plan element should define the organization during the various phases of the project, and it should define the specific responsibilities of each group within the organization. There are so many reshufflings within a large organization that when the bulletin board announces yet another, the reaction is often, "Here we go again." It's tempting to think that if we were smart enough we could organize a project once and be done with it. But there are some good reasons why we *should* reorganize from time to time:

- As the project moves along from one phase to another, the emphasis shifts from analysis to design to programming and then to system testing. The organization should shift with the work. For example, there is no need for an installation group as early as the Definition Phase, and there may be no need for a requirements analysis group during the Installation and Operation Phase.

- You should organize around the people you have. If a new manager begins working for you midway through the project, and if he has strong feelings about how his end of the project should be organized, listen to him and try to organize to suit him. Nothing wrong with that if it enhances his effectiveness and does not foul up someone else's.

• If the organization you planned for and adopted just isn't working smoothly, then, of course, change it.

Test Plan.   This section describes the tools, procedures, and responsibilities for conducting all testing levels on the project. The Test Plan should clearly define each separate level of test (for example, "module test," "integration test," "system test," "acceptance test," "site test"), responsibility for executing each level, machine support required for each level, support programs required, and the reporting of test results.

Change Control Plan.   Controlling changes in the developing program system is one of management's most vital functions. This section defines the kinds of changes to be controlled and the mechanism for effecting that control. When you write a change control procedure, it's always a temptation to try to cover every conceivable kind of change no matter how minor. Therein lies failure because these procedures quickly become so entangled in details that they become an administrative horror and collapse.

Documentation Plan.   This is a key section, but it's usually missing. Its intent is to control the gush of paper that inevitably accompanies most projects. I think one important cause of our so often getting buried under paper is that we don't take the time to define the documents we want to use on the project. As a result, whenever a project member needs to write something, he dreams up his own format and suddenly there is a new kind of document to file and keep track of. We probably need a little chaos in the world to keep us from growing too dull, but there are many better places to allow for the chaos; let's keep it out of our documentation system.

The Documentation Plan is a gathering place in the Project Plan for the descriptions of all paper work to be used during the project. When someone wants to write something down, he should be able to find an appropriate kind of document clearly outlined in the plan. If you miss a few in your initial planning, don't fret. Add new document descriptions whenever you find that they are needed. Keep your document descriptions as uncluttered and as flexible as possible so that writers will have freedom to express themselves. Since pride of authorship is a very powerful motivating force in most people, whether they admit it or not, documentation guidelines that are too restrictive will be ignored.

In addition to serving as an index of document descriptions the Documentation Plan includes a summary of publication procedures dealing with preparation, approval, reproduction, distribution, and filing.

Training Plan.   Generally, there are two categories of training required on a project: Internal (training your own people) and external (training the customer and others). Training is often awarded little or no space in a plan, but this omission can be serious on some jobs. The Training Plan defines all the kinds of internal and external training required, the responsibility for each, and the resources required.

Review and Reporting Plan.   The objective of this plan element is to define how project status will be communicated by oral project reviews, written reports, "structured walk-throughs" and "inspections."[6]

Avoid making project reviews "dog-and-pony" shows. For them to be useful you must avoid the temptation to trumpet your successes and smother the problems — a difficult task no matter how objective and honest you think you are. One way to help dig out the problems is to include competent outside reviewers, that is, people who have no personal involvement in the project. Reviews are discussed later in the text and a suggested set of reviews is included in Part II.

Written project reports, like other documents, have a way of growing more and more voluminous and less and less useful. The plan should lay out exactly what reports are required, their organization, their frequency, responsibility for writing them, their distribution, and their relation to one another.

Installation and Operation Plan.   This describes the procedure for getting your finished, "accepted" program system installed and operating properly in its intended environment, perhaps at some missile defense site, perhaps in the computing center down the hall. Even the simplest of programs can become snarled in such problems as how to convert from an existing, perhaps manual, system to the new, computerized system. These problems are discussed in Chapter 7.

Resources and Deliverables Plan.   This plan element brings together in one place the critical details associated with your plan: manpower and machine time schedules, a summary of project milestones, and a summary of all items that you are to deliver under

---

[6] Structured walk-throughs and inspections are discussed in detail later in the text. They are not intended as a means of reporting status to management, but they are an important means of helping project members assess the quality of the products they are developing.

your contract. These data are among the most frequently changed or consulted, so they should be gathered in one place to make them easier to find and easier to change.

   Index.   Not a frill, it's an effective way to make your Project Plan much more attractive and usable to the reader.

WRITING ACCEPTANCE CRITERIA

Discussion of acceptance testing is included under the Acceptance Phase in Chapter 6, but the actual work of preparing for acceptance begins here, in the Definition Phase. What deserves particular emphasis now is that the *criteria* for acceptance must be agreed to early and in writing. Don't labor through an entire project without knowing exactly what conditions your product must satisfy in order to be acceptable to the customer.

Chapter 3

The Design Phase

By now management is getting a little edgy. Weeks, perhaps months, have passed since the contract was signed, and there is still no sign of programs (in fact little sign of programmers). It's time to show the boss that everything is right on target: analysis is complete; a Project Plan has been written; the design team has been recruited and is hard at work. In short, you've met your milestones and are taking dead aim at the next set of objectives: *designing the system*, *refining the Project Plan*, and, when that's done, conducting a comprehensive *review* of the entire project before beginning programming.

DESIGNING THE SYSTEM

A key output of the Definition Phase was the Problem Specification, which defines the job to be done. The next important document to write is the Design Specification, which is the blueprint for the program system. It is the starting point for the programmers. I can't emphasize enough the importance of *having* this document and making it the focal point of the programmers' activity. Avoid playing the game that Larry Constantine, in a course on program design, called WISCA. WISCA stands for Why Isn't Sam Coding Anything? It's a ruinous game played by managers who don't understand that you must design before you code. Such managers confuse motion with progress.

The Design Specification states the solution to the customer's problem. It is a solution chosen by project management from among alternatives offered by the design team. The design chosen must be the "best" one for the project. It may not be the best in terms of elegance, nor the one chosen if unlimited resources were available, but it must be the best that can be implemented, given the constraints on available time, talent, equipment, and money. Whatever design is chosen, it must, of course, completely satisfy the requirements stated in the Problem Specification.

The Design Specification

The Design Specification describes an acceptable programming solution to the problem stated in the Problem Specification. The Design Specification is the *baseline* for all future detailed design and coding.

A good design specification shows the solution in two ways: in terms of *function* and *logic*. The functional description shows *what* the system is to do; the logic description shows *how* the system is actually structured to provide those functions. A functional description may include a box containing the words "Calculate Trajectory," but it is left to the logic descriptions to describe the method or procedures to be programmed to do the actual calculations.

Management and the designers must select the appropriate tools to use in communicating both function and logic. One method is to use HIPO charts to describe function and flow charts to describe logic. Another, more in keeping with trends in structured programming, is to use HIPO for function and structured charts or pseudo code for logic. These tools are described later.

The design documentation vehicles you end up using should be the result of investigation and reasoned decisions — don't just let something happen because of inaction. Don't let one designer use one method, another a different method. Think about how your baseline documents will interface with what preceded them (the Problem Specification) and what will follow them (the detailed program descriptions). A technique such as HIPO, for example, can be used by the analysts in writing the Problem Specification, thus smoothing the transition between that document and the Design Specification. (In fact, the *functional* section of the Design Specification may look very similar to the Problem Specification.) HIPO can, in turn, be a major part of the detailed documentation for the individual programs, thus extending the feeling of consistency and continuity in the project's technical documentation.

The general content of the Design Specification consists of the *overall design concept, standards and conventions*, the *program design*, the *file design*, and the *data flow*.

Overall design concept. This is a brief combination of narrative and diagrams providing an overview of the entire program system design at a high level.

Standards and conventions. This section states the rules adopted for use in describing both the baseline design and the detailed design to be done later by the programmers. It covers such items as flow-charting and HIPO standards, naming standards, interfacing conventions, and message formats. This section also includes *coding* standards and conventions to be observed during the Programming Phase. Prohibited, required, and recommended coding practices should be identified here. If such standards already are published for your organization, a simple reference to those standards here will suffice.

Program design. This is the core of the document. Through a combination of diagrams, narrative and tabular information, it describes the program system first functionally, and then in terms of its actual structure, or logic. It begins with a look at the overall hierarchy and then breaks the system into smaller chunks for a closer look. The level of detail must be such that no major design problems are left to the Programming Phase, but this baseline design should not be carried to the ultimate level of detail. There are two reasons for this. First, detailed design would make this a massive document, and you would find it impossible to apply effective change control. Change control must focus on the structure of the system at a high enough level that a change in the way a low-level module is coded is not subject to formal control. Second, don't make the programmer a robot who codes someone else's design. The individual programmer should be your expert at coming up with a solution (detailed design and code) that best handles a specific problem. Insist on building a solid framework for both your programs and data files and let the individual programmer concentrate on devising the best possible code to fit within that framework.

File design. This is the companion to the program design section. It defines in detail all *system files* (also called system data sets). These are files which are accessed by more than one program module. Thorough definition of these files will help you avoid a lot of misery later. Many projects have floundered because individual programmers independently designed files and later found that other programmers had had different file designs in mind and had written their programs accordingly. In one memorable case, two teams developed major program subsystems, each based on its concept of what the system files were to be like. After more than a year's work they discovered that the two subsystems were miserably incompatible because the files each assumed were worlds apart. One subsystem was scrapped; so was its manager. In my opinion, the project manager should have been held responsible. Avoiding such gross lack of communication is one of management's most urgent responsibilities.

Data flow. This is a kind of executive summary of the design, understandable by nontechnical upper management. There will be more on this later in the chapter.

The Designers

The designers must be, above all else, expert programmers, and at least some of them should have been heavily involved in the problem analysis activity. Ideally, some of the designers should be earmarked as lead programmers or managers during the Programming Phase in order to provide as much continuity as possible.

Like analysts, good designers can go quickly to the heart of a problem and not get trapped into wandering down all the little dark alleys. They must be practical; they must know what can reasonably be expected of the various components of the overall system: the machines, the programs, the people. And above all, they must communicate. I know some superb technical programmers worth ten run-of-the-mill programmers as far as technical ability is concerned, but they can't communicate. They are content and extremely productive if you carve out a big chunk of the system, define its interfaces with the rest of the system, and turn them loose. These people may be more useful in the Programming Phase than during the Design Phase.

The manager must know the technical leanings of the designers. Strong biases could easily prevent sound design tradeoffs from being evaluated. A lead designer who always tilts toward assembler language, for instance, may never give a high-level language a fair shake. Biases are inevitable, but if you know they're there, you can probably keep them from killing you.

The Design Environment

If you're an orderly person who can't stand arguments and conflict, lock up your designers and leave the room. If there's a place on a project for a little chaos, it's probably here. Don't bother them with constant interruptions, unnecessary meetings, or chores not bearing directly on their design job. Just be sure that the design effort is led by someone who has the spine and the technical competence to resolve conflicts (sometimes arbitrarily in order to get on with the job).

Design Guidelines

Designing a program system is not so mysterious as some designers would have you believe. Here are some perfectly reasonable guidelines that apply to the design of any program system, and, for that matter, any other kind of system. Good designers will observe these guidelines almost automatically.

Conceptual integrity. When designers are turned loose to design a new system, if they are any good at all, they should be full of novel ideas and clever techniques and will have an almost irresistible urge to incorporate them into the system. But if they are really good, they'll resist that urge. A well-designed system would best start with a very small number of people so that a single philosophy prevails. A good system design is not a lot of lovely limbs stuck together to make a tree; rather, it's a strong trunk which supports graceful limbs. It's up to a chief designer to assure the integrity of the system by ruling out niceties that belong in somebody else's system. He or she must keep the design squarely aimed at the system's eventual user. Brooks [37] contends that "conceptual integrity is *the* most important consideration in system design. It is better to have a system omit certain anomalous features and improvements, but to reflect one set of design ideas, than to have one that contains many good but independent and uncoordinated ideas."

Modularity. When I was a boy, I dug a lot of ditches. I went about that inspiring job in a very methodical way. First I outlined where the ditch was to go, broke loose a neat two or three cubic feet of earth with the pickaxe, and then shovelled away the loose earth cleanly so that I could now see and attack the next chunk of ditch. I always felt that I could see my progress better that way — and that little game probably helped me maintain a degree of sanity. The alternative was to whack away with the pickaxe for a longer time, piling up a strip of more or less loosened earth, and then shovel for a long time; but that way there would be fewer times when I could look back and clearly see progress.

A programming job is like a ditch. It has a beginning and (sometimes) an end. You can attack it methodically, always having a good feel for where you are, or you can lurch forward with no intermediate goal in mind except to bull your way to the end. Either way, you'll strike rocks. Mr. Neat, however, will be able to clean around the rock, see it, pry it loose, or bypass it; Mr. Bull's rock will be obscured by all that loosened earth.

Your designers should lay out the program system in chunks, or modules, not only to aid in the design process itself, but to give a big assist to the rest of the project. Modularity, that is, subdividing a job into compartments, has many advantages. I'll list them at the risk of stating the obvious.

- Modularity provides visibility. A system quickly gets so big and complicated that it's difficult to see what's going on unless we can look at it and understand it one piece at a time.

- Modules force simplicity, and as a result, less error.

- Modules are very often reusable; the more restricted the function assigned to a module, the higher the probability it can be used elsewhere in this or some other program system.

- Modules are a convenient basis for assigning work to the programmers.

- Modules are handy building blocks that can be put together in a very deliberate, controlled manner during testing, whether you are working top-down or bottom-up.

- Modules provide a convenient basis for progress-reporting and statistics-keeping.

- Modularity makes later changes easier to effect.

Module, as used in this book, is a general term applying to a clearly identified portion of the program system at any level in the hierarchy. Figure 3.1 shows a general hierarchy of modules comprising a program system. For purposes of discussion in this and later chapters, I have named the modules at each level as follows: unit, component, package, subsystem, system. The diagram simply says that the program *system* is comprised of program *subsystems* which are comprised of program *packages* which are comprised of program *components* which are comprised of program *units*. Each box in the diagram represents a program module. You may choose to call your

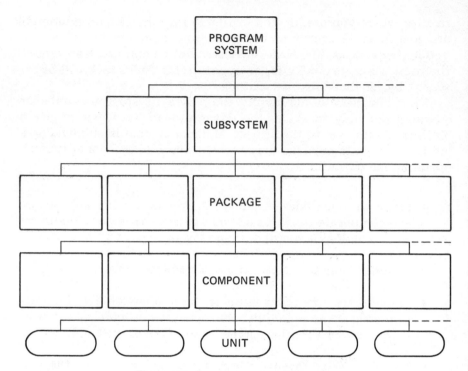

Figure 3.1. Program system hierarchy

modules at the various levels by some other names, but whatever
names you choose, use them consistently throughout the project.
You may also need more or fewer levels, depending on the nature
of your system.

The module called "unit" is the lowest level of module independently documented and controlled in the system. It's generally assigned to an individual programmer. The programmer, in coding the
unit, may break it into smaller pieces, such as routines, subroutines,
macros, or other exotic names, but when the work is documented it
is all contained in a single tidy bundle called a unit.

Interface definition. Although the designers must expend much
energy in defining the system in terms of modules, they must pay
equal attention to defining and documenting the interfaces between
modules. The Design Specification should spell out exactly how the
modules are to communicate. Programmers writing individual units
should *never* be given the freedom to combine their units in whatever fashion they wish. Flip back to Figure 2.3 for a moment (in

Chapter 2). Suppose that the ten elements in the third example are program units. Ten program units would be a very small system, yet if they were all hooked together in a different manner, there could be as many as forty-five different interfaces. Imagine the difficulty in isolating a problem in all that mess during testing (or later during operation, when the programming team is no longer around). This is not the place to give the individual programmer artistic license.

Part of the designers' job, then, is to include in the design document explicit, detailed explanations of the following:

- How modules are to communicate with other modules.

- How modules are to communicate with data files.

- How data files are to communicate with other data files, including the use of "pointers" linking one file to another.

- How human operators are to inferface with the programs; for example, how shall the operator manually enter a message selecting one of the system's options.

- How the programs are to pass data, such as error messages, to an operator.

- How the program system is to pass information to other program systems or to equipment systems such as display devices.

Simplicity. Robert Townsend [2] has this to say about what he calls "computers and their priests":

> First get it through your head that computers are big, expensive, fast, dumb adding-machine-typewriters. Then realize that most of the computer technicians that you're likely to meet or hire are complicators not simplifiers. They're trying to make it look tough. Not easy. They're building a mystique, a priesthood, their own mumbojumbo ritual to keep you from knowing what they — and you — are doing.

Sounds like he's run across some of our brethren who can't stand the English language and insist on giving their work a "professional" look by including all the hieroglyphics and fancy symbols they can squeeze in.

This tendency is often apparent in the professional journals.

Some perfectly normal people who speak clearly and usually communicate well succumb to some sort of seizure when they write an article for a journal. The subject could be dog food, but there in the middle of the article is a set of equations describing how to optimize the size of the can.

If you can find a designer who can discard such nonsense and express his design in simple, understandable language, you've got yourself a *real* professional. "It is never unprofessional . . . to make oneself clear," says Robert Gunning [5].

As program systems are asked to satisfy increasingly complex requirements, computer scientists insist that program designs become simpler. IBM's Harlan Mills, a leader in the search for better programming and management techniques, urges us to look for the "deep simplicities" in program design. Strive for modules so simple and explicit in their function and structure that they can be reused in other systems.

Simplified module coupling. We've all seen programs in which modules are strongly dependent on one another because the operation of one module depends on its "knowledge" of what's happening in the other module. In extreme cases, one module might alter the contents (sometimes instructions!) within the other. Such modules are said to possess strong coupling, and their effect is to complicate the system. Designers should aim for the *weakest* possible coupling — that is, the greatest independence — between modules. Weak coupling makes each module easier to treat as an entity, easier to design without considering its effect on other modules, and easier to alter to replace later on [36].

Minimum commitment. Larry Constantine[1] has stressed the idea of "minimum commitment." By this he means that a designer should solve detailed problems as far down in the system as possible. For example, when laying out the "package" level of module, don't give undue attention to a detail that belongs in a lower-level module, a "unit." Only express as much as you have to in a design description at any given level. Don't get hung up on details and lose track of the big things that are going on at that level.

Rule of black boxes. As a corollary to "minimum commitment," Constantine advises the designer to state a required function as a

[1] Presented by Constantine in a course on program design given at the Information and Systems Institute in Cambridge, Massachusetts.

"black box," defining its inputs and outputs with little regard for internal structure until a later pass through the design. Joseph Orlicky [6] describes the black box as a device "we simply postulate by defining its inputs and outputs." A black box, he says, *"does everything we want it to do."* Again, avoid getting so deeply involved with details that a sound basic design never shows through.

Top-down design. If you were designing a building, probably you'd start by considering the building's total environment (for example, where will it sit, on how big a piece of land, of what shape). Then you might try to determine the style of building that would fit both its intended use and its surroundings, not to mention the customer's budget and his tastes. After that you might be ready to sketch out the main structure, without details. Given tentative agreement about building height, number of floors, general shape and style, and so on, you could proceed to designing the major parts of the structure — main entries, office areas, shop areas. And then you'd get down to designing specific areas, such as offices, meeting rooms, rest rooms, shops, connecting hallways, stairwells, elevator shafts. Finally, you would need to address the placement of doors, windows, lights, outlets, plumbing, decor, and a thousand other details without which the building would not function. All through the process you would find that decisions about lower-level items would impact decisions already made at higher levels. The very tools and materials to be used in doing the job (for example, concrete or glass) might affect, and be affected by, decisions made earlier. Many iterations later, decisions would be solidified and approved (sometimes arbitrarily, in order to get on with the job). And finally the design is ready for the workmen.

The building design did not begin by concentrating on the size of the toilets, and program designs don't begin with the layout of a housekeeping module. Start with the highest, grossest, most inclusive level of functions, and refine it in ever smaller steps ("stepwise refinement") until all functions have been accounted for in a coherent and systematic manner. This is top-down design.

Top-down design is not new. It has been used by competent programmers since programming began, although the "top-down" label is more recent. The more the techniques of top-down design are used, of course, the more natural they become, and the less likely that a manager will allow his programmers to proceed in shotgun fashion. Yet, senseless as it may seem, some managers still hack a job into a number of chunks which sound sensible and then assign separate people or groups to go off and program the chunks. ("We'll worry about tying them together later; right now let's get something cycling. The customer is breathing down my neck!'') That obviously is akin to having people build windows, doors, closets, rooms, and so on, hoping later to make them fit together. Probably if a program were as visible as a window frame, we would never resort to such lunacy.

Let's remember that right now we are talking about the writing of a *baseline design*, a point of departure for the entire detailed design. The designers must decide where to stop the baseline design; this document must establish all the framework for the program system, establish all the communication conventions, and solve all the flow and control problems. The design of the individual lower-level modules, however, is left to individual programmers. There is no way to state exactly where the baseline design should be stopped; that will be different for each project, and in fact will reflect the experience, even the personalities, of the designers, managers, and programmers. As soon as the baseline design shows a complete and viable solution to the problem stated in the Problem Specification, it's finished.

Existing programs. I know very few programmers who wouldn't rather rewrite from scratch than make use of existing programs — and it's very often true that rewriting is the proper course. Making use of existing code can be a headache because of poor supporting documentation or because the code is not exactly what is needed and must be modified. Besides, modifying someone else's code is not too exciting. Nevertheless, your designers are derelict if they don't honestly consider what exists and how it may be adapted to your system. The huge operating systems and libraries of support programs built by computer manufacturers and some software houses cost hundreds of millions of dollars; there just *might* be something there that you can use. Rather than *build* a solution, you may be able to *buy* it.

Constantine, Stevens, and Meyers [*36*] make a strong case for building (at least within a given organization) program modules of such simplicity and independence that they can be used for later needs, not just to satisfy the requirements of one system or contract. The more we begin to use structured design and code, and the more we treat modules as "black boxes," the closer we'll come to realizing that goal. How many thousands of essentially identical "edit" or "binary search" or "get" or "put" routines have been built over the years?

Pity the user. Designers must constantly think and act with the total system in mind. That system includes people and machines, not just programs. You're not designing something to show how clever you are. You're building something to be used by human beings. Furthermore, those human users are usually not computer-oriented. If the computer makes their jobs easier, it may be accepted. Otherwise they'll ignore it and continue to work in their old, comfortable ways. If the computer and its complicated user's manuals are shoved down their throats, they may even sabotage the entire effort.

Rarely should a trade-off between ease of use and ease of programming be made in favor of the latter. I like what Orlicky [7] says on the subject: "Coddle the user, not the computer, and remember that the primary goal is not the efficiency of the computer system but the efficiency of the business."

Iteration. Don't think that the designers are finished the first time they have a flow chart that seems to include modules to cover all the required functions. Good design is usually the result of many iterations. Things learned while designing at the component level are bound to give the designer second thoughts about what he did at the package level. This process is repeated until the changes are minor and the chief designer calls for the rubber stamp that says *done.*

Design Tools

Most design tools are more helpful in trying out or documenting a design idea than in coming up with the idea in the first place. This is not to discount the use of such aids; it is simply to indicate that conceptualizing a design remains very much a cerebral process. Below are some of the most often used design tools, almost all of which are also helpful during problem analysis.

Flow charts. A flow chart (also called a flow diagram) is a diagram that combines symbols and abbreviated narrative to describe a sequence of operations in a program system. The symbols include such geometric shapes as boxes, circles, triangles, and diamonds, which are connected by lines indicating direction, or sequence. Each symbol has a specific meaning: a rectangle may signify a process of some kind, a diamond usually is a decision point, and so on. A few words accompanying each symbol define the operation represented by the symbol. This is one of the few places in the programming business where some degree of standardization has been achieved. The International Organization for Standardization (ISO) and the American National Standards Institute (ANSI) have adopted compatible flow chart standards.

Flow charts were once used as the primary form of documentation for almost all programs. Useful as they are, they have a rather spotty reputation. They may be much more helpful as a programmer's private thinking tool than as a formal and final means of documenting programs. As pointed out by Yourdon [35] ". . . flow charts are often a good way of organizing one's thoughts, especially during the formative stages of program design when most of one's brilliant ideas are being scribbled on the back of an envelope or some other handy scrap of paper. . . ."

Programmers are notoriously lax in keeping flow charts updated and in step with the code. It may be tempting to mutter some curses about prima donnas and vow to *make* them do it, but that's not a gainful (nor even justified) approach. More fruitful may be the use of other tools easier to update (for example, HIPO charts) and more reliance on the code itself to document the program. The use of structured code, described later, is a giant step in this direction.

Sometimes there are pressures which dictate the continued use of flow charts, even if you feel that some other tool is better. One such pressure may be customer insistence, because he is used to flow charts and gets nervous when someone rocks the boat by suggesting a change. In that case, you have an education job ahead of you.

HIPO. Traditionally, designers have laid out proposed programs using various combinations of tables, flow charts, and narrative. The flow charts have very often been a cross between *functional* diagrams and *logic* diagrams. That is, they sometimes describe the functions the programs are to perform (the *what*) and the structure, or logic, of the programs (the *how*) — all in the same set of diagrams. What is needed during the Design Phase is first a concentration on function, and then enough expression of logic to satisfy the builders and managers that not only are all functions accounted for completely, but that here is a reasonable way to build a set of programs to provide those functions. To satisfy the *functional* design, a documentation method called HIPO has been devised and is enjoying acceptance among designers, managers, and programmers. The description of logic is to a very great extent implicit in the HIPO charts, but it is left to other forms of documentation to describe logic fully (see sections on flow charts, pseudo code, structured charts, and structured code).

HIPO stands for Hierarchy plus Input-Process-Output. It consists of (1) a set of diagrams which show the functional breakdown of a program system (or any system) in the form of traditional hierarchy charts, and (2) separate diagrams which explode each box on the hierarchy chart into a set of three boxes showing inputs, processes, and outputs. Figure 3.2 shows one way of functionally representing a program using HIPO.

Each organization using the HIPO idea may use slightly different formats, but the basics remain the same. For every box shown in the overview, there is a separate chart showing the inputs to that box, the processes (or "functions" or "transformations") the box is to perform, and the outputs.

The scheme may be extended to any level of detail required to account for all functions. Normally, each box in the overview (a) will be shown in separate charts (b) as indicated in Figure 3.2. Any or all of those charts, in turn, may be further exploded, as in (c), until all functions are accounted for.

HIPO can be used effectively by other than the baseline designers. It can be used by the analysts to help express the requirements of the system. HIPO could well serve as the analysts' primary documentation. Using HIPO to express the system's requirements would ease the way for their use in describing the system's functional design. In fact, there could be a close correlation, visually and in substance, between HIPO *requirements* charts and corresponding HIPO *functional design* charts.

Furthermore, HIPO charts can be used as basic program documentation. When combined with structured code, or pseudo code and structured code, HIPO charts can eliminate the need for flow charts as a deliverable item to the customer. (See the discussions of "Coding Specifications" in Part II and in the next chapter.)

Pseudo code (or program design language). As mentioned earlier, flow charts are not always a suitable vehicle for either developing or documenting design. With the increased use of structured code for programming, a tool called pseudo code (also called Program Design Language) is used in many installations in place of flow charts to describe design logic. Pseudo code is a notation similar in look, form, and meaning to both spoken language and programming languages; it's a bridge between the two.

There is no single pseudo code. Rather, there are a number of schemes used in different organizations, tailored to both the needs of that organization and the coding language(s) used. In fact, psuedo code can take whatever form an individual designer or programmer wishes; that, however, is certainly to be avoided like plague. Pseudo code must be standardized *at least* throughout a given project, if not throughout an installation or company. If not standardized it will of course lose its value as a crisp means of communication.

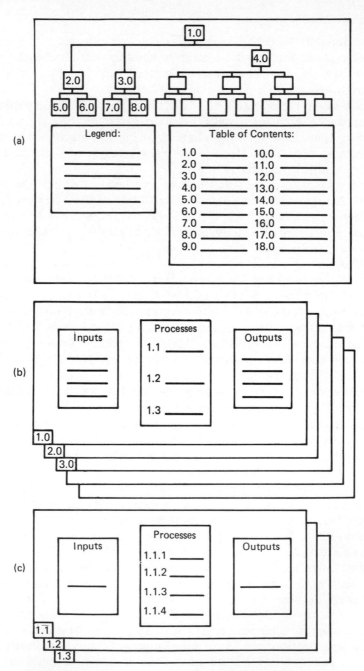

Figure 3.2. HIPO representation of program system functional design: (*a*) Hierarchy chart showing structure and brief description of each block; (*b*) individual charts showing first level of detail; (*c*) individual charts showing next level of detail

For further discussion and ideas on the development of specific pseudo code see Hughes and Michton [8] and Van Leer [9].

Structured charts. These are a pictorial way of expressing program logic, or structure, in a rigorous way, readable from top to bottom. These charts are based on the restricted set of conventions used in structured programming (see Chapter 4). There are a number of different schemes for drawing such charts. Figure 3.3a shows a set of conventions for representing each type of program structure; Figure 3.3b shows a portion of an actual structured chart where the program is to make a series of choices. Charts like those shown in these figures are often called Nassi/Shneiderman or Chapin charts, after their authors [30].

Data flow diagrams. This is a special form of flow chart, useful to both analysts and designers. Its intent, like that of any flow chart, is to use symbols and text to describe a sequence of operations, but there is a significant difference: a data flow diagram describes the system functionally but has little or no regard for the actual system *structure.* For example, in a message processing system it may be very useful to depict what happens to a message as it passes through the system: acceptance and decoding of the message; performing error checks and error corrections; extracting relevant data from the message; filing the data; updating displays affected by the message content; printing summary reports of all messages received; and eventually purging the message data from the system. These operations may be performed by several different sets of programs over a long period of time (for instance, days), with frequent involvement by human operators. Ordinary flow charts or other means of describing the programs involved may not get across a clear idea of what's happening in the system unless the reader is already very familiar with it. A data flow diagram can help illuminate the process (1) by showing *events* rather than programs or (2) by tracing the wanderings of a major chunk of *data* rather than by showing program logic.

Here is a convenient format for a data flow diagram: divide a page down the middle and show connected flow symbols down the right half of the page with the running text, or commentary, down the left half. Symbols and their explanatory text should always be kept on the same page. In this case, the text is not the abbreviated kind usually found in flow charts. Instead, it's plain English commentary describing what's happening in the diagram on the right-hand side of the page. This flow description is particularly useful to people whose main interest is in overviews.

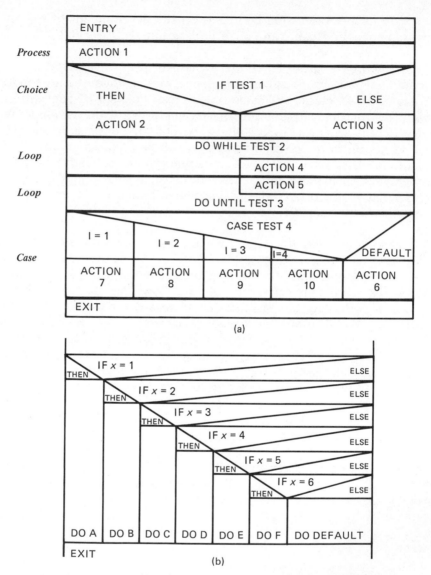

Figure 3.3. (*a*) Structured chart conventions; (*b*) structured chart example

    The symbols you use in a data-flow diagram may be quite differ-
ent from those used to describe program logic. For example, if your
system involves spaceships, radars, and display devices, you could
use symbols that represent those devices in order to make it easier
for the reader to understand the diagram.

Example (a)	Program A	Program B	Program C	Program D	Program E
Switch 1	X				
Switch 2	X	X	X		
Switch 3	X			X	
Switch 4	X				X

	Rule Numbers			
Example (b)	1	2	3	4
Request is 1st class	Y	Y		
Request is tourist			Y	Y
1st class available	Y	N		
Tourist available			Y	N
Issue 1st class	X			
Issue tourist			X	
Place on wait list		X		X

Figure 3.4. Decision table examples [3]

Decision tables.[2] A decision table is a simple, convenient way of summarizing a number of "if-then" situations. It shows at a glance what action is to be taken if a given condition or set of conditions exists. To illustrate: Example (a) in Figure 3.4 shows which program (named A, B, C, D, and E) or combination of programs must be called and executed in response to any one of four switch actions by an operator. If switch 1 is on, only program A is executed; if switch 2 is on, programs A, B, and C are executed; and so on. The table doesn't necessarily say anything about combinations of switches, but it could easily be constructed to do so. The example is very simple, but it shows some vital information at a glance. The greater the

[2] My use of the term "decision table" is rather loose, and possibly offensive to mathematicians. True decision tables are structured much more rigorously. The examples I have shown might more accurately be called "incidence tables." I have chosen to stick with the label "decision tables" as the more expressive name and because it is the term most commonly used for the type of table I'm describing.

number of switches and the greater the number of programs, the more useful the table becomes.

In example (b) in Figure 3.4 a somewhat different use of a decision table is shown. Here programs are being used to determine what kind of ticket to issue to an airlines passenger. In the table, Y means yes, N means no, and X means action. Again the example is simple, but consider how this table might be expanded to cover a more complex set of circumstances. A line entitled, "Is alternate acceptable?" might be added. Then, if first class is requested, but unavailable, and tourist *is* available, the action would be to issue a tourist ticket rather than put the passenger on a waiting list.

There is no end to the number of practical uses of such tables because they can be designed to show in one place all possible decisions for a given set of conditions. Ordinary flow charts containing the same logic might cover many sheets of paper and would be much more difficult to read. In addition, decision tables are easy to check for completeness by inspecting rows versus columns. It's much more difficult to look at a flow chart and see whether or not all required combinations of conditions have been accounted for.

Operating systems. Operating systems — programs to help manage the computer's resources — are an important part of today's computer systems. There is little question that an existing operating system, with all that it supports (assemblers, compilers, test aids, and so on) should be used as a major *tool* in developing your system. The question is, should the operating system be used also as an integral part (the control program) of the system you are producing? If you do use it, it will have a profound impact on your entire programming cycle. The operating system imposes both design and programming constraints on you, and it will saddle you with a certain amount of "overhead," or waste, that you might avoid in a tailored system. Yet, computer manufacturers have invested loads of talent and huge sums of money to produce these systems, and you may benefit greatly by adopting them even though there is always that urge to do it over again, to write a system exactly the way you want it. The big question you have to answer is whether you can *afford* not to use the existing operating system as part of your delivered product.

Coverage matrices. A coverage matrix is a means of showing the relationship between two kinds of information. An index in a book is a coverage matrix for it shows what pages in the book cover what subjects. A coverage matrix in a program design document might show system functions versus program names; that is, for a given capability stated in the Problem Specification, what program module in the Design Specification provides that capability? Such a matrix is even more useful in testing where it can be used to list functions to be tested versus identifications of the tests that are to cover those functions. One manager I worked for used a coverage matrix in another way. He listed all the items of work specifically called out in the contract down one axis and the names of the people responsible for those tasks along the other axis. The first attempt at using this matrix showed some tasks not covered by anyone. When the coverage matrix was passed among the workers, it also brought to light the fact that the boss thought person A was responsible for a particular task and A thought that task was being handled by person B.

Storage maps. These are pictures describing how the various storage devices (core, disk, tape, etc.) are being utilized. In most cases, a simple diagram showing how various blocks of storage are being used (that is, by what programs and for what purposes) is sufficient. If storage is being allocated dynamically in your system, storage maps can still be used to answer the following basic questions: Where does each kind of program reside? Where does each kind of data file reside? Where are the overflow storage areas, if any? What provisions are made for backup storage?

Programming languages [10]. The way you design may affect, and will certainly be affected by, the language or languages in which you choose to code your system. If your language is "higher-level" (for example, FORTRAN, COBOL, or PL/I), as opposed to assembly language, you may use the language itself to express some of your design. In any case, be sure to treat language selection as one of your important design decisions. Frequently a job is done in language X because that's the language this group of programmers knows best — and sometimes this makes sense. But this decision should be a positive one and not arrived at by default. Even though your programmers may be assembly language experts, maybe they should switch to FORTRAN for the current job. Or perhaps part of your job, such as a supervisor program, should be coded in assembly language and the rest in some other language. Mixing languages is often sound. If you elect to mix languages, be sure that your designers understand what interfacing problems may be introduced between the languages chosen.

Here are some questions you need to consider before you select a language for a given program:

- How frequently is the program to be executed? If infrequently, it may be a candidate for the less efficient code usually (but not always) resulting from the use of a high-level language. If the program is to be executed frequently (as in the case of supervisory programs, dispatchers, schedulers, input-output programs), it might make sense to code in assembly language. In the case of programs written to solve specific engineering problems in which a mathematical solution is sought, the choice is usually clear: use the language that enables you to code, test, and arrive at an answer in the shortest calendar time. The running-time efficiency of the program can be ignored because it's a throwaway, that is, it won't be used again once it has given an answer. (These one-shot programs, however, are generally independent and not part of a program *system*, which is our primary interest in this book.)

- Is computer internal storage an important constraint? If storage is limited, assembler code may be necessary. A given program can be coded using less core storage in assembler code than in high-level code, provided you have programmers expert in the use of assembly language.

- Is calendar time critical? If it is, and if you have a choice between competent assembly language programmers and equally competent high-level language programmers, you can probably save calendar time by going with the latter. High-level code can usually be written and tested faster than assembler code, with fewer errors.

- How competent and experienced are your programmers in the candidate languages? The answer to this may override all other considerations.

- Does each language processor you are considering support all the input-output devices necessary for this job? Careful. I know of a job in which the contract specified the use of COBOL, but the project manager learned later on in the project that COBOL did not support all the input-output devices he was using. For months the customer insisted on adherence to the contract, and he agreed to change it only after many time-consuming and embarrassing meetings and compromises between contractor and customer management at the highest levels. You can say that the contractor should have caught the error before the contract was signed and that the customer shouldn't have been so pig-headed, but the point is, *it happened.*

- Can you afford the time to train your programmers in a new language? (You should have thought of that before you signed a contract.) A COBOL programmer does not attend a two-week course in assembly language coding and emerge an assembly language expert. Can you afford his inevitable false starts?

- Is the language you have selected fully supported on all machines that you will be using? Suppose you develop your programs on one machine and install and maintain them on another, the operational machine. Unless the development machine is to be retained for making future modifications to the programs, the operational machine must include in its support program repertoire the same assembler or high-level language processing capabilities used on the development machine.

- Would it make sense in your case to code some programs first in a high-level language (to get something running early in order to test design concepts) and then later recode critical modules in assembler language? That's a luxury that may apply only to very large projects, but consider it.

These questions are intended to get you to think about alternatives. In the end, however, you must choose the language (or languages) that seems best for your job. Again, such factors as the competence and experience of your programmers may override everything else.

Simulation models. The dictionary defines a model as "a description or analogy used to help visualize something that cannot be directly observed." There are many kinds of models, including physical scale models, mathematical models, blueprints, and artists' models. Tom Humphrey, a simulation modeling expert, points out that even your desk calendar on which you jot down dates and times for appointments and meetings is a model of a portion of your life.

The kind of model of interest here is a *computer simulation model.* In this case, the system being modeled is expressed in some computer language and the computer executes the resultant programs in imitation of the described system. For example, if you are interested in a system of automated traffic control along city streets, you might describe a tentative control system in an appropriate simulation modeling language, run the model on a computer under varying traffic conditions, and determine from the model where bottlenecks are likely to occur. You can alter parameters (such as duration of red and green lights) and run the model again to see what effect your alterations have on the traffic flow.

Simulation modeling can be a powerful tool for the designer and, in fact, can be extremely helpful all the way through the project. Although it may be costly, depending on how much you want to simulate, it can pay for itself by providing the following advantages:

- Alternative design approaches can be tried under simulation before committing the project to one approach or another.

- System bottlenecks can be discovered and possible remedies investigated.

- Problems, such as running out of internal storage, can be predicted in advance so that there is time to avoid them.

- Building a simulation model to test a proposed design tends to force design completeness because the modelers must keep asking questions of the designers until the model itself is complete. The designers may, for example, forget that they have left a processing path on a flow chart dangling. The modeler, however, can't leave it dangling; he has to ask what to do about that path and in this way helps to keep the designers honest.

Assessing Design Quality

One test of design quality is obviously the degree of success of the resultant program system in meeting the customer's requirements. However, that's not enough. The program system may run perfectly and do the job intended, and yet be inadequate because it's difficult to alter to meet future needs.

Long before acceptance time, in fact *now*, before programs are actually written, managers must be able to get some handle on the quality of the baseline design. The following set of questions might be used as a starting point in assessing design quality [*11, 36*]:

1. Are all functions spelled out in the Problem Specification fully accounted for in the Design Specification?

2. Have the interfaces between the program system and human operators or machines been designed with ease of use in mind, even at the sacrifice of some programming simplicity?

3. Has the program system been broken into modules small enough to fit on a single computer printout sheet (say, 40 to 60 lines of code)?

4. Has each module been designed to perform a single specific function (such modules are said to possess "functional strength")?

5. Has each module been designed with maximum independence in mind? The best means of communication between modules is *data coupling*, wherein module A calls module B, passing to B needed data and receiving data back from B. Other means of coupling provide less module independence; for example, when module A directly refers to the contents of module B.

6. Does each module have complete predictability? Modules whose behavior is dependent on self-contained status indicators are less predictable and more difficult to test.

7. Are the rules of module-to-module communication and access to all data clearly and completely stated? Leave no room for private agreements among programmers concerning inter-module communication.

8. Is the set of documents representing the design clear, complete, and ready for further refinement and coding by the programmers?

PROJECT PLANNING

In parallel with the baseline design effort, further planning and preparation are done during the Design Phase. Most of this work falls into these areas: change control, preparation for testing, resource estimating, training, and documentation.

Change Control

The design process does not end when you have produced the Design Specification. Throughout the life of the project, and especially during the Programming Phase, changes will be proposed either to the Problem Specification or to the Design Specification, or to both. A mechanism for dealing with and controlling change is described in the next chapter. But *now* is the time to set up the apparatus. When change proposals come in, you should be ready to dispose of them quickly.

Preparation for Testing

Like most activities during the life of a project, testing must be prepared for in advance of when it will actually take place. Testing will begin during the Programming Phase; getting ready for it must be done during the Design Phase. Detailed discussion of testing is left to later chapters, but now you must set the stage.

Defining a test hierarchy. You need to define the types, or levels, of testing to be done on your project. Define them, publish them, and stick with them. I know that when terms such as "integration test" and "system test" are used, their meanings depend on who is using them. It's simply another area where clear definitions have never been agreed to. You need to be sure that *for your project* you have unambiguous definitions understood by all the project members, management outside the project, and the customer. I offer the following definitions of test levels in a test hierarchy (they are further discussed in succeeding chapters):

- *Module test.* In Figure 3.1, there are four levels of modules shown comprising the program system. Module test is the testing done on any individual module before it is combined (integrated) with the rest of the system. Module test is done by individual programmers.

- *Integration test.* Also simply called "integration," this is the process of adding a new module to the evolving system, testing this new combination, and repeating the process until finally the entire system has been brought together and thoroughly tested.

- *System test.* The integrated program system that the programmers consider clean is now run through a new series of tests; this series is *not* prepared or executed by the programmers. These new tests are run in as nearly a "live," final environment as possible, and their main objective is to test the programs against the original Problem Specification to determine whether or not the system does the job it was intended to do.

- *Acceptance test.* The program system is tested under conditions agreed to by the customer, with the objective of demonstrating to him that the system satisfies the contract requirements. In many cases, acceptance test is completely controlled by the customer or his representative.

- *Site test.* After installation in its ultimate operating environment, the program is tested once again to assure complete readiness for operation.

Top-down vs. bottom-up integration testing. Like many other aspects of the programming business, the theories and practices concerning testing have undergone a good deal of change. The changes have been both philosophical and practical.

Traditionally, a system made up of several levels of modules (suggested in a generalized way in Figure 3.1) has been tested "bottom-up." Lowest-level modules (in Fig. 3.1, "units") would be coded and tested first on a "stand-alone" basis. When the units comprising a higher-level module ("component") were ready, they would be combined and the combination tested until that component ran successfully. Meanwhile, other components would have been readied in a similar manner, and eventually appropriate groupings of components would be tested. And so on up the hierarchy, until one day — lo! a system was tested.

Top-down testing is just the reverse, at least philosophically. Testing begins with the top-level modules and proceeds down through the hierarchy. The lowest-level modules are the last to be added to the system and tested.

Either method of testing can be chosen and either will work, given adequate planning and control. But you, the manager, need to understand what's involved in each method and what's at stake in making your choice.

The first thing to understand is that the choice between top-down and bottom-up testing is a choice between two philosophies, or basic approaches. They are not necessarily mutually exclusive testing methods; each involves some of the other. For example, in using the bottom-up method, it would normally be practical or necessary to provide a framework into which the modules could be inserted for test purposes. This framework is usually a bare-bones version of the system's control program (a high-level module in the eventual system). In top-down testing, it's often necessary to code and test very early some modules (such as an output module) which have been shown at a very low level in the hierarchy. So neither approach is completely sanitary; there will generally be some mixing of the two. There's nothing wrong with that; what counts, after all, is that the system be well tested and done on time. What *is* important is that one approach or the other be selected for your project.

The approach I recommend is top-down, but later discussions in this book allow for either approach to be used. Following is a summary of the reasons for making this choice (for more detailed discussions of top-down vs. bottom-up testing, see Hughes and Michton [12], Mills [13], McGowan and Kelly [14], Yourdon [15], and Baker [16]):

- Top-down is a "natural" method; it involves building a framework before adding details.

- It fits comfortably with the ideas of top-down design and top-down coding. The whole idea of top-down development is that of a natural progression.

- As new modules in the hierarchy are added to the system and tested with the already-tested higher-level modules, the system evolves as a living, growing entity, "complete" at any given stage. Bottom-up is a more piecemeal approach, involving more finger-crossing and more surprises when groups of modules are thrown together for the first time. Surprises are for birthday parties.

- It's easier to produce intermediate versions of the final program system; effectively you have an intermediate version right from the beginning—something is cycling and showing results. This makes it easier (1) to show the customer intermediate results faster, thus avoiding end-of-project shocks; (2) to deliver interim, incomplete versions of the system; and (3) to show management that something really is being produced. Upper management has always been in the untenable position of having to accept too much on faith; it's so hard to actually see those darned programs!

- Program system integration is being continually performed as each new module is added to, and tested with, the higher-level modules already existing.

- Much less scaffolding (specially written test support code, such as dummy driver programs) is needed in top-down development.

Writing test specifications. Module testing is done by the individual programmer without a formal test document. The other four levels — integration, system, acceptance, and site testing — are performed according to previously defined test specifications. There is a separate set of test specifications for each level. Many individual tests will serve more than one test category. For example, many, perhaps all, of the acceptance demonstration tests can be taken from the set of system tests.

Figure I indicates at what point in the development cycle each specification should be ready. It's evident that if the Integration Test Specification is to be ready for use when integration testing begins, it will have to be prepared during the Design Phase; similarly the System Test Specification must be written during the Programming Phase, and so on.

Test specifications are described later. Here it's sufficient to indicate that each specification contains a definition of test objectives, success criteria, test data, and test procedures. Each specification is supported by *test cases*. A test case contains all the background information, test data, and detailed procedures required to execute one specific set of tests.

Defining test procedures. The place to allow for creativity in testing is when you're devising the tests in the first place — not when you're executing them. There will always be nail-biting moments during testing (especially during acceptance testing) no matter how well you prepare; don't add to the tension by flying blind. Write your test specifications in such a way that procedures, responsibilities, and predicted results are spelled out ahead of time.

Providing computer time. As manager, you can have significant impact on the testing process by providing the best possible access to the computers.

I suppose it might be argued that the most important aspect of computer time is that there be *enough* of it. But, assuming that the total available time is adequate, another item becomes essential: computer turnaround *predictability*. There is nothing so frustrating and wasteful of programmers' time as never knowing when a program will be run on the computer. The most frequent complaint about batch processing conditions (when a run is physically submitted to the computer facility and the programmer has to wait hours or days for it to be executed) is that the turnaround time is unpredictable. It's extremely important that a programmer know, within reasonable tolerance limits, when a program will be run and returned to him. Predictability enables him to plan his time. It allows him to lay out successions of dependent runs. It brings a measure of order to a potentially chaotic activity. Therefore, anything management can do to establish regular computer turnaround schedules will pay off handsomely.

Another way to improve testing is to pay attention to the logistics involved in getting programs and results of program runs to and from the computer. Arrange for pickup and drop stations to be close to the programmers' work areas. If necessary, supply courier service in order to speed program decks, tapes, listings, and so on to and from the computer. Make submission procedures simple. Provide ample storage for decks, tapes, disk packs, listings. Tune all computer-related services until they're working smoothly.

If you're working on a project requiring the use of classified data, do everything in your power to keep those classified data out of the computer for as long as possible. Work with simulated, unclassified data. Introduce classified material late in the development cycle, preferably not before system test. Once they are introduced, confine them to as few files as possible. Keep them *completely* out of the program modules. I've worked on several projects that required a classified (usually *secret*) data base. The complications that arise as soon as you introduce the classified material can be horrible. Any printed output is now suspect. You may argue in vain with a security officer over whether or not a given output should be classified, stamped, logged, and kept under lock. You can count on long meetings, outrageous procedures, and a great deal of slowdown in your operation once the stamp-wielders get in the door.

One more area deserving management attention is that of contingency reserve computer time, or planned idle time. In a paper on resource analysis, A.M. Pietrasanta [17] makes this comment:

> Queuing theory indicates that, as idle time approaches zero, wait time between jobs will approach infinity. The manifestation of this theory is very common to harassed programmers: turnaround time gets longer as the computing center load builds up . . . . Whatever the proper percentage of spare computer time, it is certainly unfair to demand that the computing center get rid of all idle time and still maintain tolerable job turnaround time.

Churchman, Ackoff, and Arnoff [18] describe an experiment at Boeing Aircraft that bears on reserve time. The problem at Boeing was to determine the optimum number of toolroom clerks required to service a fixed number of mechanics in the factory. Since the mechanics would come to the toolroom at an uneven rate, one clerk couldn't service them immediately and thus lines would form. At other times the clerk was completely idle.

Measurements and queuing theory were applied. It was shown that it would be economical to increase the number of clerks, *even though they would sometimes be idle*, in order to provide faster service to the higher-priced mechanics. Every time a mechanic had to wait in line, he represented lost time and lost production. It was also shown that, for a given set of mechanics' and clerks' salaries, there was an optimal number of clerks. Further increasing the number of clerks would begin to show a net loss because now the cost of idle clerks became larger than the cost of idle mechanics.

The computer serves the programmers as the clerks served the mechanics. Some idle time should be planned in order to improve turnaround, prevent long waiting lines, and improve the efficiency of all the programmers being serviced. At some point the cost of the planned reserve is balanced by the improvement in programmer efficiency.

What amount of computer resources should be planned for reserve time? There is no way of knowing without doing some experimenting, but studies in other fields indicate that a contingency reserve of about 30% might be a reasonable start. What's important is that you start with *something* and adjust the amount of reserve as you go along. Don't plan 100% utilization of the computer resource.

Plotting test results. It's useful to keep track of testing progress, especially during integration testing and system testing, by drawing simple graphs. Graphs are useful for showing trends. Suppose, for example, that you plot "test cases executed" along the horizontal axis and "test cases executed successfully" along the vertical axis. If the curve suddenly flattens out and does not rise significantly during a long period of time, that should serve as a warning that something is amiss.

Resource Estimating

As the end of the Design Phase nears, you should reestimate the resources needed to finish the job. Your early guesses about manpower and computer time can now be made more realistic because you've learned so much more about the job to be done. If your new estimate is much higher than the original, that's a problem you and the customer must somehow resolve. Better now than halfway through the Programming Phase.

Documentation

The Documentation Plan should be in good shape at the end of the Design Phase, with most documents defined and outlined. The first version of the Programmer's Handbook should now be ready for distribution, and the project library should be set up.

The Programmer's Handbook, outlined in Part II, is a loose-leaf binder containing the written information most vital to the programmer in doing his job. It includes a description of the technical requirements, the baseline design, support software, test procedures, hardware information, and a summary of the Documentation Plan. The handbook should be ready when programming begins. Its preparation and upkeep should be entrusted to a technical person, not to an administrator, because it is an important set of information for the *programmer*. Don't let it become too broad, with a section for filing every conceivable kind of document on the project. And above all, don't include in it such items as the detailed program descriptions. I've seen many a "handbook" die of bloat. Limit not only the size of the handbook but also the distribution. One or two copies for each first-level manager, kept where the programmers can get at them, should suffice. Scream, stomp, curse, and knock over your coffee when some innocent comes by asking to add two more sections to the manual and to put ten more people on the distribution list. The bigger it gets, the less likely that anyone will consult it; and the longer the distribution list, the tougher and more expensive it is to update the handbook.[3]

The project library should be fully organized and operating at the end of the Design Phase. One way of functionally organizing the library is shown in Figure 3.5 and described more fully in Chapter 4. Every item (document or program module) should be given a unique identification. Nobody but the librarian should ever get his hands on the master copy of a document or a module. This is a convenient control point for the project, but it will lose much of its value if project members are allowed free access to it. The use of the library will be discussed further in the next chapters.

[3] Many projects are reducing the need for handbooks by storing critical data in the computer and making them accessible through terminals where selected portions can be either printed or displayed on a screen, or both. A huge advantage in any such centralized library is that it can always be kept current; the often slow publications cycle is avoided.

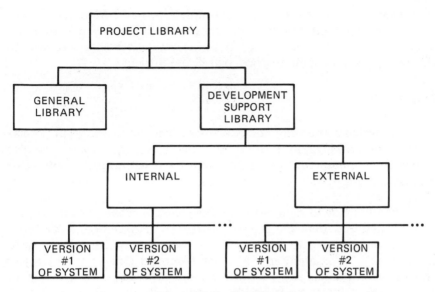

Figure 3.5. Project library

Training

During the Design Phase you should be training the programmers for their jobs during the Programming Phase. By the time the Programming Phase begins, they should all know the equipment, the programming language, the test facilities to be used, the problem definition, and the baseline design.

DESIGN PHASE REVIEW

Status reviews should be held at the end of every phase in the development cycle (see Review and Reporting Plan in Part II). Because the review held at the end of the Design Phase is probably the most critical of all, we'll look at it in some detail.

At the end of the Design Phase you're almost at a point-of-no-return. You're about to commit major resources (programming manpower, testing manpower, and computer time) and you'd better have a warm feeling that you're really ready. Once you begin implementing that baseline design, it's exhausting, expensive, and morale-busting to have to stop to do a major overhaul. The objectives of this review are (1) to assess the completeness and adequacy of the baseline design and the Project Plan, and (2) to provide management with sufficient information to decide whether to proceed to the next phase, do some rework, or kill the project.

Preparation

Don't mumble something about a review and hope everyone knows what you're talking about. State the objectives of the review and give someone complete responsibility for making all arrangements. This may be a full-time job for several days or weeks.

Scheduling people. Include as reviewers a cross-section of your own project members and representatives of management above you. In addition, be sure to invite *outside reviewers* or consultants who are not only competent in both the technical side of your project and in project management but who are also disinterested in your project. Don't invite your buddy, hoping he'll give you good marks. Give this review a chance to uncover problems. If problems are there, they will surface sooner or later, and the later they are found, the more difficulty you'll have in fixing them. For instance, a design problem might be solved in a week or so during the Design Phase. That same problem, not caught until programming is well under way, might cause a great deal of reprogramming and retesting.

Should you invite the customer? I think not. You may get into many internal problems during this review, and the customer's presence would be inhibiting. It's better to solve as many problems as possible and *then* brief the customer. This isn't double work at all, for you can treat your internal review as a warm-up for a customer review. The intent is not to hide anything from the customer but to present him with solutions and alternatives, not problems.

Choose as speakers project members who are most competent in the areas being discussed, but try to avoid starring someone who may be so glib that he glosses over problems and lulls the listeners into thinking things are in better shape than they are. I'll never forget a review session that began with a "the-project-is-in-good-shape" attitude and ended in grief. Once the good words and the pretty speeches were out of the way, one of the reviewers began asking probing questions. Shortly one of the frustrated first-level managers, in response to a question, hung his head and mumbled that there wasn't a chance of making the schedule. Shocked silence. What he had voiced was not really news to anyone on the project, but this was the first time anyone actually gave voice to his feelings. Some rapid changes followed.

How much time you need for the review depends on the size and nature of your project, the complexity of the technical problem, the difficulties you see in future phases. On a one-year project you can probably plan on spending three to five days profitably in this review. You should anticipate some prolonged discussions of problems and schedule people accordingly.

Scheduling meeting rooms. Hold the meetings as far away from your office (and telephone) as possible. If that means renting a hotel conference room for a week, do it. Arrange for frequent coffee breaks and, if necessary, for luncheons. Find a place that's air conditioned and quiet; it's tough to compete with cigar smoke and the jackhammers next door. I remember one deadly review session in which halfway through the session in a smoke-filled room a manager fell sound asleep. The speaker stopped, grinned, and silently motioned everyone out of the room. The manager was observed an hour later sneaking sheepishly back to his office.

In some cases, you may want to break people away from a main meeting room to form smaller "task forces" in order to look in depth at a specific problem. If so, you'll need to arrange for space for them. But resist the temptation to break up the group, at least until all main presentations are complete. Since this review is intended to show whether or not the whole project hangs together, the reviewers should hear all presentations, both technical and nontechnical.

Preparing presentation aids. Decide what presentation media (for example, slides, flip charts, chalkboards) will be used and make sure that the appropriate equipment is available for each presenter. If some other group is to help you prepare charts and slides, find out how much lead time they need.

Preparing handout materials. Be very selective about what you give the reviewers if you expect them to read it. The two documents that they should surely get are the Design Specification and the Project Plan. Beyond that, it's up to you. Whatever you hand out, make sure it's clean and readable. Send the documents to the reviewers well in advance of the actual meeting.

What to Cover

I've already stated that the general objectives are to review plans and the baseline design. Figure 3.6 suggests an outline of review topics you might use. The section on *Background* should give the reviewers a feel for the environment in which you are working and a general idea of the technical problem as well as your proposed solution.

Under the *Project Plan* heading, present at least a capsule description of each plan section and a more detailed look at the Phase Plan, Organization Plan, Test Plan, and Resources and Deliverables Plan. The *Baseline Design* section should describe in increasing levels of detail the design you have produced. It may be a good idea to break for a day or so, once a first level of detail has been presented. This will give the reviewers a chance to absorb what they have heard, look through the design document, and then return better able to hear

```
I   BACKGROUND

    A.  The Customer
        • his experience
        • your prior experience with him
        • his organization

    B.  The Job
        • reason for this project
        • job environment
        • overview of requirements
        • overview of design

    C.  The Contract
        • overall schedule
        • costs
        • major constraints

II  THE PROJECT PLAN

    A.  Overview
    B.  Phase Plan
    C.  Organization Plan
    D.  Test Plan
    E.  Change Control Plan
    F.  Documentation Plan
    G.  Training Plan
    H.  Review and Reporting Plan
    I.  Installation and Operation Plan
    J.  Resources and Deliverables Plan

III THE BASELINE DESIGN

    A.  Program Design
    B.  File Design
```

Figure 3.6. Design phase review outline

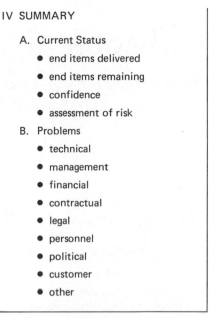

IV SUMMARY

A. Current Status
- end items delivered
- end items remaining
- confidence
- assessment of risk

B. Problems
- technical
- management
- financial
- contractual
- legal
- personnel
- political
- customer
- other

Figure 3.6. (Continued)

more detail. The *Summary* presentation should paint an honest picture of where you think you stand and what major problems you face. Distinguish between problems you feel you can solve and problems requiring your management's help.

Results

What you want from the review is the go-ahead to get on with the job. In most cases it will be clear when the review ends what kind of shape you're in. In other cases, you or your management will insist that certain problems be solved before programming can proceed.

When you set up the review, ask certain participants to be prepared to put in writing their opinions of your project's status, their listing of your outstanding problems, and any suggestions for dealing with those problems. Encourage reviewers to state what they see as problems even if they have no suggested solutions. You should solicit these written comments from each outside reviewer and from selected project members. Their comments should be given to your management along with your own recommendations. (Every review should end with a formal written report from you.)

At the conclusion of a successful review, or after making changes as a result of the review, the green light is on and the Programming Phase begins.

Chapter 4

The Programming Phase

At last you're ready to write programs, and things begin to happen. Suddenly there are more people to manage; the paper pile has swollen; programmers can't get enough computer time; flaws show up in the baseline design; the customer leans on your programmers to bootleg changes; your manager says you're overrunning the budget; Jack programmer is a dud; Jill programmer gets married and leaves; and your spouse is bugging you about being married to that stupid computer. You'll be thankful you planned and designed well because your hands will be full tending to daily problems that no amount of planning can avert. This chapter focuses on the programming job and the most effective way to get it done.

STRUCTURED PROGRAMMING

The way many programs have been built is akin to erecting a skyscraper by turning loose a bunch of workmen who proceed to dig into their favorite jobs. One decides to build the thirteenth floor, another begins styling elegant doors and windows, a few poor souls attempt to lay in a foundation, and, of course, some snob goes right to work on a penthouse.

Structured programming is an effort to establish order in the construction of a program. There is a good deal of hesitancy on the part of most computer scientists and programmers in defining structured programming. Many define the term by saying what it is *not:* it is *not* a "bowl of spaghetti" approach; it is *not* a "rat's nest" approach;

it is *not laissez-faire* for the programmer; it is *not* cute and tricky code; and so on.

According to Yourdon, "the notion of structured programming is a *philosophy* of writing programs according to a set of rigid rules in order to decrease testing problems, increase productivity, and increase the readability of the resulting program" [19]. Hughes and Michton offer this: ". . . we could say that *structured programming* is 'the design, writing, and testing of a program *in a prescribed pattern of organization*'" [20].

Harlan Mills says ". . . the essence of structured programming is the presence of rigor and structure in programming. . ." [13].

The ideas that are common to all the definitions of structured programming are order, clarity, and readability, all leading toward the goal of error-free code which may be readily understood by people other than the program's author. The days of intricate secret code written by snobs or messy code written by poorly trained programmers are, we may hope, coming to an end. There is such a strong drive among the leaders of the programming community to bring order to the business that sooner or later the entire complexion of the programming activity shall certainly change for the better. The transition from the old ways to the new is, of course, most difficult for those accustomed to the old; setting new programmers on a clearer road, before they have learned bad habits, is relatively easy.

Goals of Structured Programming

Let's look more closely at some specific goals of structured programming.

Correctness. Nobody wants to structure programs simply to make them pretty. What counts in the end is that the programs be correct—that they do their prescribed functions flawlessly. Using structured programming and related concepts, complex programs are now being written which run correctly the first time. A book you and your programmers should consider must reading begins:

There is an old myth about programming today and there is a new reality. The old myth is that programming must be an error prone, cut-and-try process of frustration and anxiety. The new reality is that you can learn to consistently design and write programs that are correct from the beginning and that prove to be error free in their testing and subsequent use.

By practicing principles of structured programming and its mathematics, you should be able to write correct programs and convince yourself and others that they are correct by logic and reason rather than by trial and error. Your programs should ordinarily execute properly the first time you try them, and from then on. If you are a professional programmer, errors in program logic should be extremely rare, because you can prevent them from entering your programs by positive action on your part. Programs do not acquire bugs as people do germs — just by being around other buggy programs. They acquire bugs only from their authors. [21]

We may hope that one day no programmer will ever again slap together some code, ram it into the computer, and pray. Instead, he may be expected to program in such a manner that it would be a genuine and unwelcome surprise should the code not operate correctly the first time.

Readability. There is no place in today's computer business for programs which cannot be read by other than the original authors. In the past we tended to excuse such code as the work of either a genius or a dud. If that of a genius, many managers felt technically inferior and incapable of challenging such practices, or afraid of losing their "star" performers by presuming to question their programming practices. If a dud, the programmer might be nudged into "fixing up" the programs after the fact (or someone else might be assigned that onerous task). Any way you look at it, this results in a patchwork job and loss of time, manpower, money, and customer confidence.

Programs must be made readable *from the start* so that they can be inspected by managers, supervisors, and other programmers who are double-checking logic or tracking down problems in the system. Programs must be readable *at the finish* so that they can be modified and maintained by other than the original programmers.

Testability. It follows that a readable, clearly structured program may be more easily tested (especially by someone other than the original author) than a mysterious program.

Increased productivity. Improvements in the first three goals (correctness, readability, testability) automatically lead to lower programming costs.

Techniques of Structured Programming

Detailed structured programming techniques are beyond the scope of this book, but an introduction to them is in order. I urge you to study full treatments of the subject. Some excellent sources, which in turn refer to many additional readings, are Hughes and Michton [8], McGowan and Kelly [14], Yourdon [15], Baker [16], and Linger et al [21].

The essence of structured programming can be summarized as follows: All coding is forced to follow a strict set of conventions which eliminate all or most unconditional branches and cause individual programs to be developed in a logical sequence, formatted to make the code easier to read. The result is a program readable from top to bottom, from beginning to end. The code, complete with supporting comments, should be self-descriptive. How is this accomplished?

First, most of the need for unconditional (*go to*) branching in source code is eliminated by the adoption of certain coding conventions. There has been considerable controversy over whether *all* such branching can be eliminated. The answer is partly dependent on the language currently being used (some lend themselves more readily to the elimination of such branches, some make it difficult or impossible) and on the nature of the application. Nonetheless, there is general agreement that most of this kind of branching can and should be eliminated. Where there are recognized needs for exceptions, individual organizations set up strict rules governing those exceptions.

Elimination of unconditional branching means that, as one reads down a program source code listing, there is a continuity which is not destroyed by a branch to the far country, never to return. I remember trying to solve a programming problem on the now-ancient SAGE computer and encountering a BPX instruction (essentially an unconditional branch) which had mysteriously appeared after the latest compilation. When asked about the BPX, the programmer shrugged, "It was only a *little* BPX." So help me!

What are the coding conventions, aside from eliminating or restricting the use of little BPXs? In a paper which became the basis for much current work in structured programming, Böhm and Jacopini [22] proposed that a program, any program, can be written using combinations of only three program structures:

1. *Process*

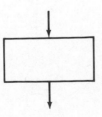

2. *Choice*
   (IFTHENELSE)

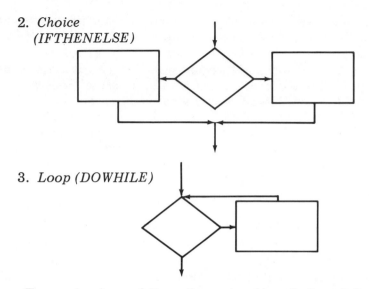

3. *Loop (DOWHILE)*

Two extensions of these three structures 1, 2, and 3 commonly accepted are DOUNTIL, a variation of DOWHILE, and CASE, a variation of IFTHENELSE. They may be represented as follows:

4. *Loop (DOUNTIL)*

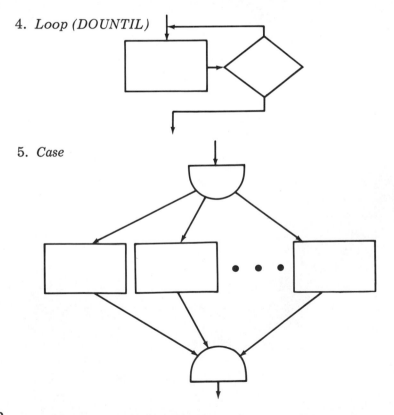

5. *Case*

There are variations to the method of depicting these operations, and they may be implemented in different manners within the various programming languages (FORTRAN vs. COBOL, for example). But the impact is the same: programs can be constructed using combinations of these structures which, in the program listing, read from top to bottom and tell a straightforward story without the confusion of disruptive branches.

In addition to the rigorous use of the these structures, structured code is written according to strict but sensible rules of indentation and alignment. The effect is very similar to that of a table of contents, where indentation and alignment show logical groupings of chapter titles and subheadings.

ORGANIZATION

There are a couple of basic ways of organizing people to do a job. One is *functional* organization. Essentially, this means that you borrow people from groups of specialists within your company. Each specialist is on loan to you to do his part of the job, and then he's gone — on loan to the next manager who needs his skills. This arrangement gives you, the project manager, little control because the man on loan to you is likely to be more concerned with his home organization than with your project. Typically, you have little or no say about whom you get, and you can be frustrated by substitutions made before your job is finished. Perhaps worse than that there will be little or no continuity of people on your job. In the worst case, the analysts come, they analyze, they leave. The designers come, they design, they leave. And the same for the programmers.

Another kind of organization is the "job-shop." To use it, simply break up the program system into several major subsystems and assign a manager and his group total responsibility for developing that subsystem — analysis, design, programming, the works. I attacked a job that way many years ago and regretted it long afterward. Here the problem is that nobody has his eye on the *system* because the managers are concerned only with the *sub*systems. A job-shop arrangement works if you are doing a number of relatively small, unrelated jobs (in other words, *not* a system). If you're a manager accustomed to a job-shop organization and are about to manage the development of a system, remember that what worked before may not work now.

Neither functional nor job-shop organization is appropriate for producing a system. The kind of organization needed here is *project* organization. What is implied in any such arrangement is that (1) the people involved devote their efforts to a single project; and (2) they are all under the control of a single project manager.

Project organization may take many forms. Every company has its rules about lines of authority, degree of autonomy, reporting to outside management, and so on. Such considerations aside, however, we may discuss project organization in terms of two quite different approaches: *conventional* and *team* organizations.

CONVENTIONAL ORGANIZATION

Figure 4.1 illustrates two conventional ways to organize your forty-person project. The only real difference between (a) and (b) is the number of management levels between you, the project manager, and the people who do the technical work. The choice of (a) or (b) depends on your strengths and weaknesses and those of the managers who are available to you. If you are technically strong, able to absorb much detail, and can handle as many as seven managers reporting to you (a hefty number), then (a) might well be your choice. The danger here is that you may become swamped in details, lose sight of broader project objectives, and lose control. If you prefer to delegate more responsibility so that you can concentrate on the important problems that arise, then (b) might be your choice. In that case you have four managers reporting to you. Either way your project has many managers (seven or eight besides you), and that may horrify your boss ("Where are the workers!?"). As I hope to show, these managers are not paperwork shufflers. Since they are very much involved in technical decisions, the ratio of managers to workers is not so bad as it looks.

I think in most situations I would choose (b) over (a). The real importance, however, is not in the exact number of boxes on the organization chart nor their titles but in the fact that you must account for all jobs that have to be done and do it in a workable way. Then you must be sure that every member of the organization knows both his and other people's objectives. Given that, you're off to a good start.

The remainder of this section describes the functions of the various groups shown in Figure 4.1b and ends by considering some typical numbers of people in the various roles.

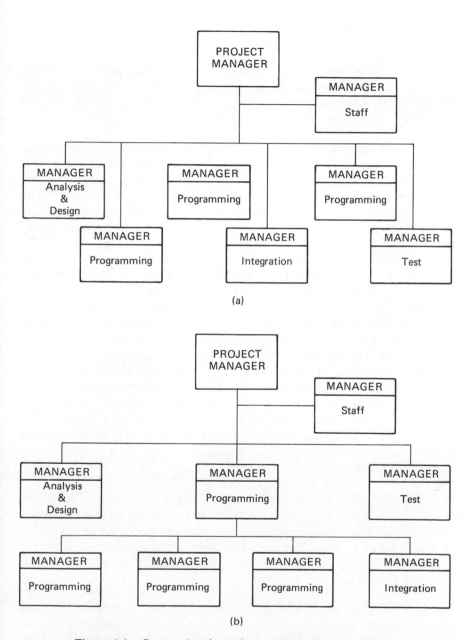

Figure 4.1. Conventional project organization, programming phase; (*a*) Two levels of management; (*b*) three levels of management

Analysis and Design Group

Remember that you're now in the Programming Phase and, therefore, the programmers are at center stage. However, the analysts and designers still play a very strong supporting role. A subset of the original analysts and designers have the following jobs to do:

Controlling change. The most important function of this group is to carry out the change control procedures described later in this chapter. This boils down to investigating proposed changes, recommending adoption or rejection, and documenting the results. The group acts as a filter. It relieves other project members, particularly the programmers, from much of the burden of digging into a proposed change and tracking down the consequences of making the change. On many projects the investigation of a change proposal falls on the programmer. He is constantly sidetracked from his main job to run down this or that idea suggested by the customer or by someone in his own organization. When a person is doing something as logic-oriented as programming, every interruption means a loss of efficiency. When the interruption ends, he must say, "Now, where was I?" In addition to the wasted time backtracking, he may well end up with a bug at the point of interruption. Very often the frustration of constant interruption causes the programmer to give a hasty answer and to agree to the change just to get the problem off his back so that he can get on with his programming. Those hasty answers will return to haunt you. Having a group handle change proposals concentrates a vital function in one place rather than spreading it thinly over the project.

Data control. This is really part of the change control function, but it needs emphasis. Data control means keeping an eye on all system files so that their structures are not violated. By "system files" I mean those organizations of data that are accessed (either stored into or retrieved from) by more than a single program module. System file structures, a dictionary defining each data item, and all the rules for using system files, should have been spelled out as part of the baseline design. In a great many program systems these data files hold the system together. Just as it is necessary to control changes to program logic after the baseline has been established, so too must changes to the system files be controlled. Don't leave it to the programmers to form *ad hoc* agreements as they go along.

Structured walk-throughs and inspections. The Analysis and Design Group is a good place to assign responsibility for scheduling and
conducting continuing detailed reviews of technical progress. There
are two closely related means of conducting such reviews: *structured
walk-throughs* and *inspections.* Both these terms came into use during the 1970s; some people make a distinction between the two,
some use the terms interchangeably.

A structured walk-through is simply an organized (structured)
review of a project member's work by other project members.
During a walk-through, the developer (the person whose work is
being reviewed) first gives a tutorial description of his project (which
may be a design, code, a set of documentation, a test plan, or any
other item). Then the project member "walks through" the product
verbally, step by step, giving the reviewers a "guided tour" and inviting them to find flaws. The vehicle the developer uses may be whatever is appropriate to his product. If a design is involved, then HIPO
charts and other design documents would be pertinent; if a module
of code is involved, then the actual code would be used — or pseudo
code if the actual code has not yet been written; if reviewing a test
plan or user's manual, then either a detailed outline or a draft version
of those documents would be walked through. The idea is that there
be a definite, very specific look in detail at each product rather than
relying on the testing process to show up problems or simply passing
documents around with "buck-slips," hoping that people will review
and comment on them.

There are generally four to six participants in a structured walk-
through. One of them is always a *moderator.* Since I'm suggesting
that the Analysis and Design Group be responsible for scheduling and
conducting the walk-throughs, I believe a member of that group
should act as moderator. The moderator schedules the meetings and
meeting places, helps select participants, reports results immediately
after the meeting, and follows up to see that any rework to be done
is done and presented again if necessary. But most important, he
must keep the walk-through sessions moving along toward their
objectives without getting sidetracked and without allowing animos-
ities or bruised egos to destroy the effectiveness of the review.

The other participants in the walk-through include the developer
whose work is being reviewed, and two to four others who are competent enough to understand his work and its place in the system. If
the work being reviewed is a module of code, one of the participants
might be a programmer responsible for similar code or code which
interfaces this module directly; another might be a programmer

responsible for code elsewhere in the system, say, in the control program. If the module was designed by someone other than the coder, the original designer should be present.

As you can see, the makeup of the review groups can be quite flexible. The moderator must select reviewers thoughtfully. In most cases, managers are not included in walk-throughs. These sessions are not intended as vehicles for appraising employees; a manager's presence would inevitably put a huge damper on the proceedings.

The aim of the walk-through is to find errors, not to correct them. Corrections must be assumed to be within the province and capabilities of the developer.

A review session might last for fifteen minutes to two hours. If more than two hours is needed, a second session can be scheduled after an appropriate break (probably later in the same day, so that continuity is not lost).

There are some extremely important benefits as a result of conducting serious and frequent walk-throughs of all the project's products:

1. Where the product is actual design or code, there is a demonstrable and significant saving when errors are found early. The later in a project's life an error is found, the greater the cost of fixing the error. A good deal of expensive, time-consuming regression testing might have to be performed to ensure that making a change to fix an error embedded deep in the system will not adversely affect other code already tested and presumed clean.

2. There can be an enormous benefit in promoting what's called "egoless programming" (or egoless anything, for that matter). In an excellent book all programming managers should read, *The Psychology of Computer Programming* [38], Gerald Weinberg makes a strong case for taking steps toward making the programmer less defensive about errors in his work by promoting the idea of programmers reading each other's code in order to find problems. He cites evidence that a great many bugs never see the computer when code reading is practiced. The advantages go beyond that, however. Extensive and regular reading of code provides a beautiful opportunity for helping to train newer people, and the process fosters a feeling of openness on the project, in direct contrast to the situation in which a programmer treats a module of code as his own private property.

3. When the product is a document, say a test plan or a user's manual, savings are effected not only by avoiding errors in those documents which might affect the testing or the use of the system, but by cutting down on republication and distribution costs, as well.

4. Frequent and productive walk-throughs, once they become an accepted way of project life, lead to better products in the first place, because developers will not knowingly submit sloppy work for such scrutiny. It's very common for a programmer or a writer to throw together a "quick-and-dirty" first hack at a program or a document, intending to "clean it up" later. But often, later never comes. Walk-throughs can go a long way toward eliminating such sloppy and dangerous habits.

5. There is an enormous educational benefit as a result of walk-throughs. It becomes impossible for individuals to work for long periods in isolation from other project members, with their work hidden from scrutiny. Everybody knows what everybody else is doing.

The term "inspection" is preferred by some over "structured walk-through" to denote a similar but much more rigorous activity [23]. Inspections are more intensive examinations of detailed design and code, with much more emphasis on keeping statistics on types of errors found to help guide subsequent inspections. The rigor and careful record-keeping of inspections become important as projects grow large and loss of control becomes a problem.

Simulation modeling. The Analysis and Design Group is responsible for continuing simulation modeling activities begun during earlier phases. It conducts simulation runs and evaluates and distributes results. It may propose design changes as a result of some simulations. On a very large project in which much simulation is done it may be necessary to form a separate simulation modeling group.

User documentation. User documentation includes anything you are responsible for writing that will help the customer to use the system. (The other major category of documentation is *descriptive*, something telling how the system is put together. That's the programmers' job.) User documentation may include the following topics:

- Installing the system.

- Periodic testing of the system after installation.

- Daily start-up procedures.

- Daily operating procedures, options, and error correction.

- Preparing inputs for the system.

- Analyzing outputs from the system.

This is a job that requires much assistance from the programmers, but it should be the responsibility of analysts and designers since they presumably have a better understanding of the customer viewpoint. On some projects, the user writes these documents with the assistance of the Analysis and Design group.

Programming Groups

The programmers are the focal point in the organization. Their job may be thought of as a series of five steps: detailed design, coding, module test, documentation, and integration. The individual programmer is responsible for the first four and he at least assists in the fifth.

Detailed design. The programmer inherits from the designers the document called the Design Specification. This is the *baseline* for all his work. The programs he writes must mesh perfectly with the baseline design; otherwise, either his program or the baseline design must change. The individual programmer is assigned a piece of the baseline design by his manager or supervisor. Let's assume that this is a single module. His first job is to design the module in detail, living within all the rules laid down in the Design Specification. The programmer's vehicle for expressing this detailed design is the document called a Coding Specification (described in Part II). The programmer is expected to devise the best detailed design possible, consistent with the baseline design. Violation of the baseline design is a capital offense. Off with the head!

A problem arises. Some programmers have no use for detailed

design documents. They would rather code directly from the baseline design and skip the detailed design. Other programmers would rather code first and design later. What to do?

First, I think it's a fair assumption that someday someone will need to modify your program system. In order to do so that person will have to understand it and will require detailed documentation. Unless one of these assumptions is false in your case, you'll need Coding Specifications. The next question is *when?* Must they be done *before* coding? Clearly, if our only concern is for the customer who might later modify the programs, the answer is no. All the customer cares about is that the detailed design documents be delivered with the programs. He doesn't care whether the documents are written before or after coding (as long as they're accurate). If the customer doesn't care, who does? *You* should, for the following reasons:

- The Coding Specification is the only vehicle to use in reviewing the programmer's work before it gets too far into coding and testing.

- It's the only reasonable document to use in continuing design review.

- Writing a detailed planning document forces a better product.

- If for any reason a programmer leaves your project, you'll be better off with a decent Coding Specification than with a half-coded, undocumented program module.

Despite these arguments, you may occasionally allow coding to be done directly from the baseline design. Some portions of the baseline design may have been done in sufficient detail to allow this. Like everything else on the project, if you go that way, make it the result of a reasoned decision. Don't just shrug and let it happen.

Coding. This is the translation of the detailed design into computer instructions. As coding proceeds, changes in the detailed design will often be found advisable or necessary. Making these changes is the responsibility of the programmer, except when the baseline design is affected.

A manager should watch for programmers who have a penchant for writing unnecessarily tight, complex code. Although there will be times when it will be necessary to save every bit and every microsecond possible, there usually are much more important considerations. For example, code should be readable by another competent programmer. I can cite more than one instance when a pseudoprofessional programmer left behind a batch of code that worked but was unintelligible to anyone else but the programmer. In one case, the programmer left a marvelously efficient major program, but one day it became necessary to modify that program. The unsuspecting manager promised the customer that the modifications would be done and delivered in four weeks. *Six months* later, the job was not done, and the embarrassed manager finally had to have the program rewritten from scratch. An extreme example? Not at all. Watch out for it. Here simplicity pays off. If you want to challenge your programmers, challenge them to write efficient code that even *you* can understand.

Module test.[1] This is the process of testing an individual module in an isolated environment *before* combining it with other tested modules. The objective is to determine that this module when inserted into the system, will do its job as a black box. It should be capable of accepting its specified inputs and producing exactly the right outputs.

Although the project may supply various test aids, module testing is the programmer's job. I do not suggest imposing any rigid, formal module test scheme — only general guidelines. The programmer should put on paper, in his own words and in his own format, the steps he proposes to execute in order to test the module. He should discuss this informal "module test plan" with his manager, subject it to a walk-through, modify it if necessary, and execute it.

Module-testing may involve no more than thorough desk-checking and clean compilation; a step further would be to "walk through" the code with another programmer. Many modules will need to be tested further in a "stand-alone" manner — that is, not yet combined with other system modules — by providing test data and test drivers (programs whose purpose is to supply a special test environment for the module).

Decisions concerning the nature and extent of module test will be influenced by whether you are testing top-down or bottom-up. In bottom-up testing, drivers of various kinds would normally be used to represent the "top" of the system — that is, the part of the program system above the module in the hierarchy and responsible for

---

[1] Ordinarily, an individual programmer would be assigned what I have earlier called a "unit," the lowest-level module in the system; it might follow, then, that this discussion should be about "unit test." Often, however, the lowest-level module in a given path will be at some higher level than "unit," perhaps what I have called "component." In those cases, the term "unit test" would be incorrect. My use of "module test," then, is an attempt to be more general.

invoking the module in the first place. In top-down testing, the "top" of the system already exists. The module can be added to the existing system. What needs to be simulated in this case is any relevant module below the one being tested. In this case, the programmer writes code called "stubs" to stand in for the missing lower module(s). Stubs, generally simpler than drivers and test executives, may simply record that they have been called and return control to the invoking module. Stubs may go further and simulate the actions that will eventually be taken by the real modules for which they are temporarily substituting.

The most efficient way to provide stubs is to build the entire system of stubs in advance, rather than have them introduced by individual programmers as they are needed. As new modules are completed and inserted into the system, corresponding stubs can be deleted.

Documentation. "Document unto others as you would have them document unto you," say Kreitzberg and Schneiderman [*34*]. Good advice. Here is where an otherwise good product may be poorly represented. The programmers are responsible for the documents that describe in detail how the system has been constructed. The vehicle they use is the Coding Specification (see Fig. 2.1 and also the Documentation Plan in Part II). This is the same document the programmer used to show his detailed design before the module was coded. When the module has been tested, its Coding Specification should be corrected and completed by the addition of the machine listing of the actual coded module. Thus, the original Coding Specification showed detailed design intent, and the completed document shows *final design* along with resultant code. The logic and the code described in the Coding Specification should be completely accurate and consistent. The connective tissue tying all the individual Coding Specifications together is the Design Specification. That combination should completely and adequately describe the program system structure.

Integration: top-down. Integration, or integration testing, is the process of gradually adding new modules to the evolving system and testing to assure that the new module and the system perform properly. Let's assume you've chosen top-down integration testing as your project's approach, consistent with your use of top-down design and top-down structured programming. How to proceed? There are several avenues:

1. All integration testing could be done by a separate group (see Fig. 4.1) whose sole function is just that. The members of the

group would not themselves actually write any of the programs. Individually tested modules would be turned over to this integration test team. The team would add each module to the developing system and test it according to a predetermined integration test plan.

2. All integration testing could be done by individual programmers (eliminate the "Integration" group in Figure 4.1). Each programmer would be responsible for adding his modules and running tests according to the test plan.

3. Integration testing could be handled by a group which also has programming responsibility. Logically, this would be the group charged with writing the higher-level modules in the program hierarchy — the "executive" program, "control" program, or whatever you name the set of code which serves as the system's framework.

It seems to me that the third alternative is generally best. This choice guarantees that the people responsible for integration have the most intimate knowledge of the overall system. Choice (1) is workable, perhaps even best, for large projects, where there are so many programs involved that integration is a huge task. But keep in mind that a separate group with no part in the actual programming may be too far removed from the system. They would be in a less favorable position to spot problems and devise solutions; and they might be less motivated, since they have no code of their own at stake. A strong counterargument, of course, is that such a separate group could be more objective, for the very reason that their own code is *not* under question. Choice (2) invites chaos.

Integration: bottom-up. As tested modules become available from the programmers, the process of integration begins. Theoretically, this means that units are combined and tested together to form components; these components are grouped and tested to form packages; and so on up the pyramid (see Fig. 3.1) until the complete system has been put together and progressively, exhaustively tested. In practice, you will usually find that no matter how neatly you lay things out on paper, the process is not quite that clean and orderly. One reason is that some "components" will be ready while other "units" are still being coded; another is that when bugs show up at each level of test, buggy units have to be sent back to the drawing board for more work. Nevertheless, integration testing should be planned as an orderly building process allowing for detours.

There are at least two ways to proceed with bottom-up integration. One is to have programmers produce the lowest-level modules, that is, units, and turn them over to a separate group for integration. Another is to have the programming groups integrate their portions of the system and turn their work over in much larger chunks to a separate group. The first way may be theoretically more attractive, but the second way is more practical and vastly more satisfying to the programmers because it gives the individual programmer more responsibility than to simply keep producing small parts (units) for someone else to assemble.

As in the case of top-down testing, the group responsible for integration also could be responsible for writing the basic control program for the system. It will be necessary during earlier test planning to decide at what level work done by the Programming Groups will be turned over to the Integration Group. For example, you might give your Programming Groups responsibility for detailed design, coding, module test, documentation, and integration up through the *program package* level (see Figure 3.1). When integration of an individual package has been completed, the package is turned over to the Integration Group for final merging of packages into subsystems and subsystems into a system. You may, of course, choose a different level at which to submit modules to the Integration Group.

Integration: the test specification. Since the Integration Test Specification is key to the formal testing process, let's look at it in a little more detail. (An outline is included in the Documentation Plan in Part II).

The Integration Test Specification must be ready to use early in the Programming Phase, when integration actually begins. The document must, therefore, be finished during the Design Phase (see Figure I). It describes test objectives, general procedures and tools, and success criteria, and it includes a coverage matrix showing which specific tests (or "test cases") cover which functional areas of the program system. It is required whether top-down or bottom-up testing is used.

The Integration Test Specification calls for a number of *test cases.* A test case contains the detailed objectives, data, and procedures required for a given test. A look at the coverage matrix mentioned earlier should show which test case or cases apply to a given functional area.

The key items in a test case are the *data* required for the test and a *script.* A script (often called a scenario) is a set of step-by-step procedures telling, for this test, what is to be done, who is to do it, when it is to be done, what to look for, and what to record. Similar scripts are described in the next chapter in which system testing is discussed.

Tacking test cases onto a basic test specification, rather than writing one huge testing document, is another example of modularity. It's so much easier to see where you are when things are done in clean, finite chunks. And going back to repeat a test is simple when you can point to a single test case and say, "Do it again."

Figure 4.2 illustrates four formal test specifications that I'm advocating here and in the next two chapters. Each has the same conceptual organization. In fact, as the figure shows, certain test cases may serve equally well during integration testing, system testing, acceptance testing, and site testing. Good planning early in the project will enable you to maximize the multiple use of test cases.

I've asked integration test programmers on many projects what they wished they had done differently after the job was all over. Invariably, they reply that they wished the tests had been carefully laid out in advance so that when integration time arrived they could concentrate on running the tests, evaluating results, and making fixes. It's too late to begin test planning when testing actually begins. All you can do then is fumble and pray that baseline designing and module testing have been done so well that things fall into place easily.

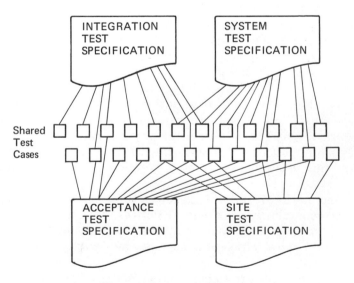

Figure 4.2. Test specifications

Test Group

During the Programming Phase, the job of the Test Group is to get ready for system test, acceptance test, and site test. *This is not the same group responsible for integration test.* Its orientation is quite different. Whereas the integration testers were concerned with putting program modules together, testing interfaces, and testing both system logic and function, the system and acceptance testers are almost solely concerned with testing *function.* They are not directly concerned with the structure of the program system. They *are* concerned with how the program system performs and how well it satisfies the requirements stated in the Problem Specification. The Test Group comes into prominence in the next two chapters, but they must prepare *now*, during the Programming Phase. During this phase their job includes: writing test specifications; building specific test cases; predicting results; getting test data ready; making tentative arrangements for computer time; setting up test schedules; organizing test libraries; choosing and securing test tools.

Staff Group

Some technical people look at staff groups as hangers-on, paper-pilers, drains on the overhead, and general pains in the neck. Occasionally that view is justified, for some managers surround themselves with so many assistants of various kinds that it's difficult to determine who is the manager. This happens in big organizations because rules, regulations, and associated paperwork get out of hand and staff people are hired to control them. Some staff people create more rules, regulations, and paperwork, causing the disease to spread rapidly. This occurs even in smaller organizations, particularly when the *customer* happens to be big. For example, if you deal with the federal government, the amount of paperwork needed to conform to government regulations can be enormous. An RFP (Request for Proposals) issued by the Department of the Army, is a case in point. (Essentially, an RFP is a statement of a job the customer, in this case, the Army, wants done. Prospective contractors study the document, find out whatever else they can about the job, and bid on it.) This particular RFP was approximately three inches thick: about one-third was devoted to describing the job to be done; one-third included appendices; and the remainder contained descriptions and lists of government regulations to which the proposal had to conform. This last third was a killer, and the immediate reaction to it was horror. The next reaction was, "Well, we can't change the government (at least not overnight) and we can't ignore these regulations or we'll lose the job." Result: all kinds of staff people were hired to handle all the requirements stated in those regulations, and before we knew it we had an organization in which only a handful of people actually did the technical job but they had an army of support. A familiar situation.

What stands out in my observation of staff groups is that after a while no one knows why they're there, let alone why they were originally formed. A manager often takes on a staff member to work in an area but doesn't really define that person's job. The result is that his job overlaps five other people's jobs. If the staff member is industrious, he will define his work scope and very soon will generate requirements for more staff help. If less ambitious, this person will do a specific job that consumes 20% of his time and then spend the rest of the time wandering the halls. There's only one way I know to avoid amoebalike growth of staff functions: you must define the staff member's job as clearly as you would define a programmer's job. Surely you wouldn't hire a programmer and tell him to find a piece of programming work to do. You'd say, "Here's the overall job, here's the piece I'd like you to do, here's the schedule, and this is how I want you to report progress." Do the same with a staff member. Don't hire one unless you can assign specific responsibilities.

The two kinds of staff functions that you're likely to need on your forty-member project are technical and administrative.

Technical staff functions. The people supplying technical support must themselves be technically competent. Their function is to focus on tasks that help all the other technical people on the project. Their specific jobs are:

- *Controlling computer time.* All computer time needs should be funnelled to one person who should secure the time each week, schedule it as equitably as possible among those who request it, resolve conflicts, observe priorities, keep accurate records of time requested and used, plan for time needed weeks and months ahead, and dispense the aspirin when time is cancelled. I had this job on one project, and I like to think it worked well. Since everyone on the project knew that there was one person to go to for computer time, many potential conflicts were avoided. On a specific day each week, I requested that the computer time needs for the following week be given to me. I would then juggle requests against the amount of time available for that week (always too little) and make up a tentative schedule in grease pencil on a big plastic wall chart. Everyone had a day or so to look at the charts and squawk. (I tried not to clobber the same guy two weeks in a row). Then I put the schedules on paper, passed them out, and that was it for the week. Although there were sometimes modifications during the week, the system worked well.

Part of this job is to set up and enforce the rules for use of computer time. The staff member should write the procedures (crisply and clearly) for submitting remote runs or for "hands-on" use of the machine, arrange for pickup and delivery of test runs and computer outputs, and provide for such physical facilities as bins and cabinets and for courier service if necessary. In short, this person should be the interface between the computer installation and its users.

- *Supplying keypunch services.* The same staff member responsible for computer time should also supply keypunch service. He should estimate the amount of service needed and arrange for it (I'm assuming that the actual keypunch service is not a part of your project), take care of incidental problems such as the need for special keypunch character sets, determine priorities whenever necessary, and get a keypunch machine (perhaps several) for exclusive use by your programmers when they require immediate turnaround.

- *Coordinating programming terminals.* If you're using programming terminals (that is, devices connected to, but remote from, the computer that allow programmers to enter code without visiting the computer), a technical staff member coordinates the planning and installation of these devices.

- *Maintaining the Programmer's Handbook.* Organizing the handbook, getting it distributed, and keeping it updated should be done by the technical staff. The handbook is discussed in Chapter 3 and is outlined in the Documentation Plan in Part II.

- *Training.* Unless training is a very large function for your project, the Staff Group should be responsible for both internal and external training and should provide for instructors, training facilities, written training materials, schedules, and training cost estimates.

- *Handling special technical assignments.* Occasionally, there are specific, short-range technical jobs to be done, but there's no specific place to assign them. For example, there may be a troublesome problem that cuts across several of your groups and must be tracked down. I suggest that you include someone in your staff estimates to allow for this fire-fighting.

Administrative staff functions. I began this section grumbling about various staff groups getting out of hand. One such group is the administrative staff. Before I list its specific functions, let me say what an administrative staff is *not:* First, it's not project management; it's an aid to project management. Second, it's not a quality control department; quality control is a management function, and quality will not be assured by having ten thousand administrators looking over the programmer's shoulder and filling out forms and reports. Third, it's neither a personnel management group nor a salary administration group; those are management jobs. The functions of the administrative staff *are* as follows:

- *Document control.* This is as vital a function as any on the project. If documentation goes careening out of control, the project will wind up on the sick list. The administrative staff has the job of handling documentation as laid out in the Documentation Plan. The job includes: setting up and operating the project general library; handling all interfacing between the project and any outside technical publications organization; keeping track of document numbers and issuing new ones on request; publishing a periodic documentation index listing the names and numbers of all project documents; providing for all reproduction services and equipment. A specific document controlled by the technical rather than the administrative staff is the Programmer's Handbook.

- *Report control.* The staff assists you by gathering status data and drafting status reports from you to your management and from you to the customer. It also obtains and distributes to you and all managers on the project periodic financial status reports. The staff prepares a final report, the Project History described earlier. If PERT or other automated report and control systems are used on the project, the staff prepares its inputs (from data obtained from line managers) and distributes its outputs.

- *Contract change control.* When a contract change has been agreed to on a technical level, the staff handles the job of completing the paperwork showing that the customer formally agrees to the change. Part of the job is assessing the cost of the change. In doing this, the staff will coordinate among four parties — the technical people who make the first estimate of cost, you, your company's financial and legal services, and the customer.

- *Secretarial and typing support for the project.*

The Numbers Game

Figure 4.3 is identical to Figure 4.1b but with two pieces of information added: a summary of the jobs of each group and numbers of people in each group. The numbers are, of course, subject to argument and will vary from one project to another, but I'll briefly give my rationale for choosing the numbers shown in each box.

Project manager. Of *course* there is a "one" in this box — what else? Well, there are sometimes two people. The second is called an assistant project manager or some other meaningless term. Avoid having two because it makes it difficult to know who's responsible for what.

Staff. One manager and seven workers. The seven are three technical staff members and four administrative workers. Among the administrative members are three secretaries. The remaining administrative member, along with the group manager, handles contract matters, documentation control, and report preparation.

Analysis and design. Three workers plus the manager should be sufficient to handle the functions I've described. Toward the end of the Programming Phase, the number may be reduced, or more likely, the group may merge with the Test Group in order to help perform system test and acceptance test.

Test. During this phase, the Test Group's main responsibility is getting ready for system test, acceptance test, and site test. Four people should suffice.

Programming. I've shown three relatively small groups — small compared to the group sizes often seen on actual projects. Indeed,

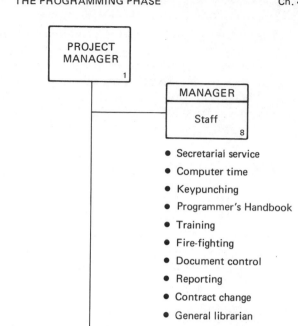

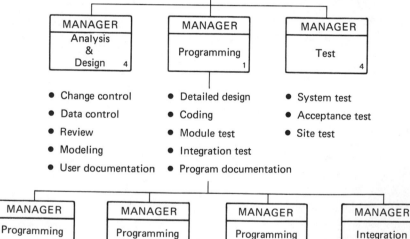

Figure 4.3. The numbers game

all the groups in this organization are intentionally small. The job of a first-level manager is tough. If you define this person's job the way I do late in this chapter, you shouldn't give him ten or twelve or twenty people to manage and then expect a first-rate job. Keep this group small enough that the manager can become intimately involved with the details of the work. Working with a horde, you can expect this person to become a paper shuffler.

If you are doing top-down integration, the group of four called "Integration" could be labelled "Programming." It would be responsible for the high-level system modules *and* for integrating the work of the other groups with its own.

TEAM ORGANIZATION

The team approach is a way of organizing around a group of specialists. The embodiment of the approach in programming is called the Chief Programmer Team.

IBM's Harlan Mills, originator of the concept, compares the Chief Programmer Team to a surgical team, where a chief surgeon plans and performs an operation with vital help and backup from highly skilled assistants, both surgeons and nonsurgeons. Dr. Mills, a prime mover in this as well as many other modern programming innovations and improvements, played the role of chief programmer in a now well-known experimental project [24] to write a program system called Definitive Orbit Determination. The goal was to have a single expert programmer, Mills, produce the DOD system in six months with the aid of a supporting team; the task had been estimated as a thirty man-year job for a conventional programming group. The task finally took about six man-years to complete, more than the stated goal, but far less than the conventional estimate.

In a second project, soon after the Mills experiment, IBM applied the team concept, along with top-down development and structured programming, to the *New York Times* project. This was an actual contract calling for the automation of the newspaper's clipping file to allow users to scan a large file of abstracts of articles. The full text of an article, stored on microfiche, could be retrieved and displayed at a number of terminals.

The finished system consists of more than 80,000 lines of source code. It took eleven man-years of effort over a period of twenty-two calendar months. Both the productivity attained and the strikingly low-level error rates are discussed by the project's chief programmer, F. Terry Baker [25, 26]. Examples of the error statistics:

- Only twenty-five errors of any kind during the first year of operation after acceptance.

- An average of one detected error and 10,000 lines of code for each of the project's principal programmers.

- Twenty months of operation before an error was discovered in the file maintenance subsystem.

In both these projects, the then-new concept of a Chief Programmer Team was used with notable success. Since then, it has been refined and applied to many more projects, especially within IBM's Federal Systems Division, as well as elsewhere in the programming community. What follows is an overview of how this idea is put into practice.

How It Works

The core of a Chief Programmer Team would normally be three people: a chief programmer, a backup programmer, and a technical librarian.

The *chief programmer* is the technical manager responsible for the development of the program system. This person will normally write at least the critical "system" modules — that is, the portion of the program system exercising control over, and interfacing with, all the lower-level "working" modules. Depending on the total size and complexity of the job, he and the backup might write the *entire* program system. Where others are involved, the chief programmer assigns work to them and integrates all their modules with his own. The chief programmer is the main interface with the customer, at least in technical matters (there may be a managerial counterpart who handles nontechnical tasks).

The *backup programmer* assists in any way assigned by the chief programmer, but his primary function is to understand all facets of the system as well as the chief programmer does and to be ready at any time to take over as chief programmer. The backup programmer is normally assigned specific portions of the system to design, code, and test, as well as other duties — for example, preparation of a test plan.

The *technical librarian*[2] is responsible for running the Development Support Library. This person is a full and vital member of the

---

[2] I use the term "technical librarian" to distinguish between this person and the "general librarian" who runs the project's general library and has the normal responsibility usually associated with a library.

team, not on part-time loan from somewhere else. The librarian's duties include preparing machine inputs as directed by the programmers (he or she may type or punch inputs or have them done elsewhere); submitting and picking up computer runs; and filing all outputs.

This team of three may be augmented by other people, such as programmers who are specialists in a given area or less senior programmers who code a specific portion of the system designed by the chief or the backup programmer. There is no sure limit to the size of such a team, but six to eight, by consensus and experience thus far, seems to be the top of the range.

The idea of the Chief Programmer Team was born as a result of the search for better, more efficient ways of producing complex programs free of errors. Mammoth undertakings, such as IBM's OS/360, had made clear that ways must be found to dramatically improve the quality and to reduce the cost in future software development efforts. The thrust of the team concept is that those goals of quality and efficiency can be achieved through a very tight, disciplined organization of a small number of highly motivated people very experienced and skilled in all aspects of program development, from analysis down through design, code, test, and documentation. In keeping the number of people small, the human communication problems (and therefore the *program* communication problems) could be drastically reduced. Just compare the possible interfaces among, say, six people as opposed to thirty!

But simply choosing top people and organizing them in a small group is not enough. They need better tools with which to work. These tools, in the case of the early experiments with Chief Programmer Teams, were:

- Development Support Library.

- Top-down development, including design, code, and test.

- Structured programming.

These same tools are now recommended, of course, *whatever* the organizational structure.

As the Chief Programmer Team concept is tried by more and more organizations, it will inevitably be refined and will lead to other ideas and tools. One natural outgrowth is the use of a "team of teams," where a large problem is broken down in a hierarchical manner, and major subsystems assigned to individual teams which are responsible to a "higher-level" team which is in turn responsible for the system as a whole.

Your Project

Suppose you are to use the team approach on your project. How might the total organization look, and how would the various functions be handled?

Your organization might look something like Figure 4.4a, which shows a little more than half as many people as under conventional organization. Numbers here are not very meaningful, since we're not discussing a job of known size. For a given system, you might be able

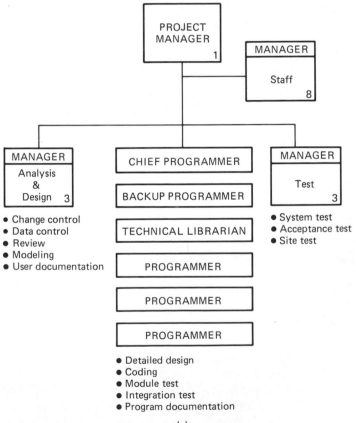

(a)

Figure 4.4. (*a*) Team project organization, programming phase; (*b*) alternate team organization

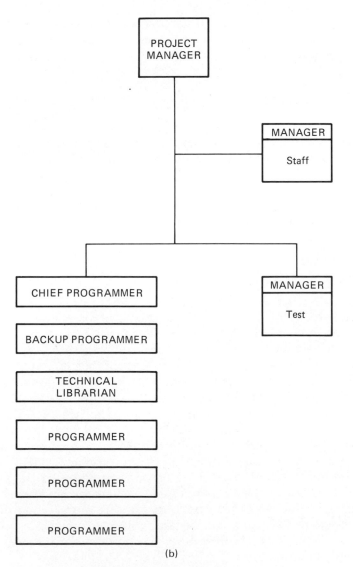

(b)

Figure 4.4. (Continued)

to eliminate half the Staff Group, all of the Analysis and Design Group, and some of the Test Group, as in Figure 4.4b. Those functions might all be handled by the Chief Programmer Team.

The answers concerning numbers of people depend not only on the nature and complexity of the job, but on the talents of the people comprising the Chief Programmer Team. The team approach assumes highly skilled and dedicated team members, but there is nothing quantitatively fixed about those terms. How highly skilled? How dedicated? There is nothing about the team approach to relieve management from making critical judgements and decisions.

CHANGE CONTROL

Choose your change control procedure thoughtfully. Too much control will suffocate you; too little and you will drift. Don't build a change control empire in which there are volumes of procedures describing how to handle any conceivable change. Think about the critical items over which you really need control, and leave the rest for day-to-day management action.

Baseline Documents

First, you must decide what to control against, that is, what are the things you want to use as foundations, or baselines. I suggest two baseline documents: the Problem Specification and the Design Specification. If you put your effort into making these two documents fine pieces of work in the first place and set up your procedures to control changes to them, then it's hard to go wrong. Conversely, if your baseline documents are shallow and poorly done, or if you fail to control changes to them, it's hard to go right.

There is a third kind of baseline you may need to consider. The two mentioned above are established early in the development cycle and are used to guide production of the program system. If you are responsible for maintenance or for more versions of the system beyond the initial delivery, then the *delivered program system* becomes a new baseline. In other words, in working on a second or third or nth version of the program system, you may use the last delivery as the baseline. Here, however, we will discuss only a single-delivery development cycle.

Control Procedures

If we agree on controlling change against the Problem Specification and the Design Specification, we can now consider a simple control mechanism that you can tailor to fit your needs. Whenever an individual sees a need for a change that he thinks may affect one of the baselines, he proposes a formal change. The Analysis and Design

Group analyzes the proposed change and recommends adoption or rejection. The recommendation is then submitted to the Change Control Board which makes its decision, subject to override by either you or the customer. The Analysis and Design Group documents the decision, and the change, if adopted, is implemented. Now let's take a closer look at how this procedure might work.

Proposing a change. Anyone, either in your organization or the customer's, can propose a change. To do so, a simple Change Proposal form is filled out that describes the need for the change, and, if possible, the way to make the change. As a rule, a programmer proposes a change only if he thinks one of the baselines might be affected. A Change Proposal is not submitted every time a piece of detailed design for a module is slightly altered.

There is one kind of change that falls outside this formal control procedure, but it must be mentioned in passing. Suppose a programmer wants to make a change to one of the modules already submitted for integration test. The change affects neither the Problem Specification nor the Design Specification, but it does affect the detailed design — the Coding Specification for the module. The change might be to correct a late-found bug or to improve a piece of code. Whether or not to accept the change in this case should be up to whoever is in charge of integration testing involving that module. If the change makes sense, it should be accepted only in the form of a new copy of the program module, a corrected Coding Specification, and an updated module identification. *No change* should ever be accepted without a change in the module identifier. Every time you let one through you lose a little more control.[3]

Investigation. All proposed changes are investigated by the Analysis and Design Group. One investigator is assigned to any given proposed change. He scans the proposal to get an idea of its importance and impact, and then schedules it for a decision at a future meeting (usually the next scheduled meeting) of the Change Control Board. If the change is urgent, a special meeting may be called as soon as the investigator has enough information to make a recommendation.

The investigator looks into all pertinent aspects of the change, writes down a recommendation, and gives a copy to each member

---

[3] The objection may be raised that there is no time for this. It may seem that way, but you will always spend more time chasing problems caused by uncontrolled code changes than you would have spent controlling the changes in the first place.

of the board within a reasonable time (say, two working days) before the board is to meet. Each investigator's report should include:

- A summary of the proposed change.

- The originator's name and organization.

- Classification of the change (Type 1 or 2) as determined by the investigator (see below).

- The impact of the change on costs, schedules, or other programs.

- A recommendation for or against adoption.

Kinds of changes. The investigator may put the change into either of two categories: *Type 1* if the change affects either of the baseline documents or would cause a cost, schedule, or other impact; *Type 2* if the change affects neither baseline and has negligible cost, schedule, or other impact. Be sure that changes don't too easily become categorized as Type 2, when they really do cost something and ought to be Type 1. Don't be "nice guys" and allow the project to be nibbled to death by too many Type 2 changes.

You can make things a lot more complicated, but don't. There's no sense inventing a dozen different change categories to cover combinations of situations. Either the change will cause some problems (Type 1) or it's no sweat (Type 2). Even the ponderous machinery of the federal government's Configuration Management gets by with only two categories of change. Surely you don't want to be put to shame by the world's greatest bureaucracy!

Change control board. The board should be comprised of representatives from various project groups. At periodic meetings (say, once a week) the board should consider all scheduled change proposals. The board discusses each change and decides how to dispose of it. You'll have to decide whether your board will operate democratically by voting on each issue or whether it will allow the chairman to make the decision after hearing the arguments. Democracy is great, but you may find things move much faster if you give the chairman the power to decide what the board's recommendation should be. You can always overrule if one of the other board members convinces you that a particular decision was a bad one. (Don't overrule too often or you'll destroy the chairman.)

The Change Control Board should be comprised of the following:

- Chairman: the manager of the Analysis and Design Group. He's got to be tough, fair, technically sharp and politically savvy.

- Permanent members: the manager of the Programming Group, the manager of the Test Group, and the manager of the Staff Group.

- Others: the investigator for the proposal being considered; technical personnel invited by any of the permanent members.

At any board meeting, then, there will be at least five participants — four regular members and one investigator. It's important not to let these meetings get too big by inviting too many extras, but obviously if there is someone who can shed more light on the proposal than anyone else, that person should be present. Often this will mean that the person who proposed the change will be there.

Should the customer be invited to board meetings? Generally, yes, although there may be times when you would rather not have him around. For example, the customer should be excluded whenever company proprietary data are to be exposed or discussed. The best way to handle this question is simply to level with the customer. Then he can be invited whenever the coast is clear.

Types of recommendations. If the board agrees with the investigator that a change is a Type 2, the change should be automatically accepted and no further board action is necessary. If it is a Type 1, it must recommend to you how to dispose of the change. There are two possibilities:

- Acceptance of the change and an indication when the change should be made (immediately or in some future version of the program).

- Rejection of the change.

Customer directed changes. Some changes will be insisted on by the customer. They must still be investigated, considered by the board, their cost and impact estimated, and formally approved by the customer. It is always the customer's right to override any decision by the board, provided appropriate contract changes are negotiated.

Implementing a change. Depending on the board's recommendation for a Type 1 change, two concluding actions are possible. If the board recommends rejection, the proposal is logged as closed. If the board recommends adoption, the investigator writes up a summary of the change, its cost, and the schedule for making the change; the package is then given to you for your signature. You sign it, and if there is a cost or schedule impact, you send the package to the customer for approval. When the customer approves it in writing, the investigator finally distributes to all concerned a written description of the change. Now the change can be implemented by the programmers.

The above is the *formal* procedure. There will be many instances when a change cannot be held up for days or weeks. Here you speed up the process by investigating immediately, calling a quick, special board meeting, writing out the recommendation in longhand, approving it verbally, getting the customer's agreement verbally and telling the programmer to go ahead. *But,* make sure that the formal paperwork follows — customer's approval, change notice, and so on. Otherwise, you'll soon lose track of things.

Periodically, the board chairman should give you a summary list of all changes considered, the board's recommendation in each case, and a very brief statement of the main arguments for and against. Then if you spot something with which you think you disagree, you can have the item reconsidered.

The Analysis and Design Group is also responsible for keeping track of a schedule for all changes. On many projects changes come thick and fast. Some are designated for immediate implementation; some are deferred to some specific later version of the program system. It's important that everyone — you and the customer — know exactly when accepted changes will be made.

PROGRAMMING TOOLS

Tools for doing the programming job must be selected before the Programming Phase actually begins. Some tools, such as operating systems, simulation models, HIPO, pseudo code, structured charts, flow charts, decision tables, and coverage matrices, were mentioned in the last chapter. Useful as analysis and design tools, they continue to serve as programming tools, as well.

The following are brief descriptions of other tools that you should consider during programming. Some of them are programs, some are hardware, and some are simply documents. In larger projects (see Chapter 8) it is often necessary to have a separate group of people to provide the rest of the project with suitable programming aids.

Written Specifications

In Figure 2.1, I outlined three key documents: Problem Specification, Design Specification, and Coding Specification. Earlier in this chapter I mentioned another document called an Integration Test Specification. Because these tools are so important they deserve repeated emphasis.

Problem Specification. This is written by analysts during the Definition Phase. It's a baseline; it describes the problem that your project is all about.

Design Specification. This is written by program designers during the Design Phase to describe the overall program system, the solution to the problem. It is also a baseline that sets the stage for all ensuing *detailed* design.

Coding Specification. These specifications are written by programmers during the Programming Phase. Each specification describes in detail the design for a portion of the overall system laid out in the Design Specification. Coding is done from these specifications.

Integration Test Specification. Written during the Design Phase, this specification describes the objectives for integration testing, and spells out specific test procedures and test data for reaching those objectives.

Test Executives

Most program systems include some form of control program, or *executive.* In bottom-up testing, a test executive is a modified version of the eventual full executive program. It begins as a simplified, perhaps only a skeletal, form of the ultimate program. It's written early to provide a framework for integration testing. Some test executives contain "dummy" modules or "stubs," that are gradually replaced as their "real" counterparts emerge from module test. The stubs may do little more than record and print an indication that they have been invoked. Or they may perform some simple operation in imitation of what the real module will do when it is eventually inserted into the system. As stubs are replaced by real modules, the program system begins to take shape. In top-down testing, the test executive is essentially the code for the higher-level ("system") modules.

Some test executives contain special test aids that are removed during the final stages of integration test. One such test aid may be a trace program to keep track of sequences of events within the system for later analysis. Another aid is a program to provide displays, or "snapshots," of key computer registers or storage areas at strategic times.

An example of a test executive used in the early stages of development of "real-time" systems is a non-real-time version of the system's control program. Similarly, a single-processor control program is often written prior to development of a full multiprocessing capability.

A test executive can be complex, but as a rule it should be kept simple for two reasons: First, its value lies partly in having it ready *early*, before the "real" executive program is finished. If you put too much into the test executive, it won't be ready much sooner than the real one. Second, the more complex you make the executive, the tougher it will be to separate *its* problems, or bugs, from those of the modules that you are trying to test.

Environment Simulators

An environment simulator is a program that temporarily, for testing purposes, replaces some part of the world with which your program system must eventually interface. For example, suppose you are writing a program system for directing air traffic. One of the pieces of equipment with which your programs must eventually communicate is a radar set. But because the radar is still being developed, or because it's not yet feasible to hook up to it, you may need to develop programs that "look" like a radar. These special programs would attempt to simulate both the radar's inputs to your operational program system and the radar's responses to your outputs.

Other simulation programs might replace special display consoles still under development. Still others might be used to feed your system sets of data representing real-world operational conditions; in our example operational conditions might be traffic loads or weather information. To be most effective, an environment simulator must be *transparent* to the using programs, that is, your programs should require little or no special modification in order to communicate with the simulators. Your programs should think that they are dealing with the real world. Any change you make to allow your program system to run with the simulator lessens your confidence that the system will run properly when the real thing is substituted for the simulator.

Depending on the size and nature of your job, your environment simulation programs may operate in the same computer as do your operational programs, or the simulators may run in a separate computer that interfaces with yours.

The cost of developing environmental simulators can be enormous. In the air traffic control job suggested above, the cost of the simulators could easily be greater than that of the operational programs themselves. The need for these tools must be addressed in the Definition and Design Phases. The simulators require the same care in design and programming as do the operational programs.

Automated Documentation Aids

You'll need to find out what automated aids, if any, are available in your company or from your computer manufacturer. There are a good many systems which purport to automate the drawing and updating of flow charts, for example. If flow charts are to be a part of your documentation, these aids may be worth considering. If you consider using an automated system, make your decision early. It's expensive, wasteful, and aggravating to decide halfway through a project that you're going to switch to an automated system.

In addition to automated charting, there are a number of excellent systems for automating the preparation of text, whether programming documents or simple memos. These generally involve combinations of typewriters and simple computers. Such systems are extremely useful in writing documents that evolve and change a good deal; they're a real boon when you have lots of form letters to write, where only the addressee changes.

Programming Terminals

There was a time when programmers did all their assembly, compilation, and debug work right at the computer console. I can remember some horribly long sieges back in the 1950s when I was working on the SAGE air-defense programs. My buddy and I sometimes hogged an entire computer site (and there were *two* computers at each site) for twelve-hour blocks. We sat at the consoles to track down bugs by single-stepping through hundreds of instructions over and over again, occasionally stopping to insert new instructions into the machine by flipping banks of external switches. Those were the days when you briskly kicked a card reader in order to cure an unexpected halt in the system. It was all great fun then, but it was extremely wasteful. Times really have changed. Now there is less and less "block time" and more sharing of computers through complex operating systems — programs that reside permanently in the computer and regulate the use of the computer system's resources. And as operating systems make the programmer's presence at the computer console less and less necessary, inevitably there begins a search for ways to make better use of this forced remoteness. Better logistics between the programmer and the computer (that is, getting card decks, listings, and so on, back and forth more efficiently) are one answer, of course. Another is to use programming terminals.

Programming terminals are various hardware devices remote from the computer but electrically connected to it. There are many different kinds of terminals, but most of them offer, as a minimum, some form of input device (such as a keyboard) and an output device (such as a display screen or a typewriter). Some operating systems include support for these terminals by allowing the programmer to use the same languages and test features previously available to him through ordinary batch processing. Some systems include terminal features not previously available at all. For example, the programmer may sit at his terminal and develop, execute, and modify a program. He can start and stop a program, make on-the-spot changes, and inspect and change data values at whatever point he wishes during program execution. Obviously, whether to orient your program development around terminals is an important project decision.

Terminals are being used extensively by managers as well as programmers. Data relating to the technical status of the developing system, or simply accounting or resource data, are stored for retrieval by managers via terminals.

Software Monitors

A software monitor is code added to a system for the purpose of inspecting and gathering data at key points during execution. A highly successful example is the Statistics Gathering System (SGS) used years ago in the Apollo program at Houston. Data gathered by SGS during operation of the Apollo system showed the developers a great deal about the execution times and frequency of operation of key modules. These data were also used to calibrate and improve the accuracy of the Apollo simulation models.

A software monitor might be a large effort, as in the case of SGS, or it might amount to inserting a few small routines at critical points in your program system to take counts of module usage.

Hardware Monitors

Some manufacturers offer for rent or sale hardware devices that may be attached to a computer to make certain measurements. Most of these monitors are intended to give you data to help determine how efficiently your system is utilizing various input-output channels or how your system's workload is divided between computation and input-output activities.

The Project Library

A library is an organized collection of information. Your project's library should consist of two sections: the general library and the Development Support Library (see Figure 3.5).

General library. Keep master copies of all project documents in this section, other than those in the Development Support Library. A basic list of documents to include:

- Project Plan.

- Problem Specification.

- Design Specification.

- Test Specifications.

- Technical Notes.

- Administrative Notes.

- Change Documents.

- Test Reports.

- Status Reports.

- Project History.

- Forms.

- Documentation Index.

In addition, keep a copy of the modules and documentation for any previous version of the system you have completed and delivered.

Every document in the library should be given a unique identifying number by the librarian. The librarian should have quick access to reproduction equipment and be able to run a copy of a master document when requested. He should never let the master out of his hands. He may keep on hand a number of copies of often-requested documents rather than run them off only on request. The librarian should keep a log of document numbers so that when any project member is ready to issue a new document in some category, for instance, a Design Change Notice, he need only call the library to get a unique document number.

Periodically, the librarian should send out a new Documentation Index. This is a printed listing of all documents currently in the library. The listing should show document titles, authors, dates of issue, and identification numbers.

The librarian should also periodically gather *vital records* and store them in a facility physically separate from your facility. Vital records are whatever materials you decide are necessary in order to reconstruct your system if a fire or other catastrophe were to wipe you out. Vital records might include a taped copy of your program system as it stands at some instant in time, along with a copy of the specifications describing the system at that time. It costs relatively little to do this job, and it can save you a lot. One project during the 1960s had made no such provisions. The programs were being developed in a "fire-proof" building at an Air Force base in Florida. The system was nearly completed. One night the building was gutted by fire and practically everything was lost — cards, tapes, listings, the works. And, of course, no other copy of the system existed. The story has a happy ending because the programmers had enough bootlegged listings in their homes to piece the system together again. Contract saved, payment made.

Development Support Library (DSL) [16, 27, 28]. Included among the important innovations and improvements in the programming process is the Development Support Library (also called by other names, including Program Support Library and Programming Production Library). The DSL is the project's central storage place for the official version of the developing program system. It consists of two sections, *internal* and *external*, and procedures governing their use.

The *internal* library contains, on disk, tape, or other computer storage, the programs being developed and data relating to their development. Exactly what is stored depends on the nature of the project and especially the computer system being used, but typically the internal library would include the most current source code and object code for all modules in the developing system, test data, control language statements, and so on.

The *external* library consists of listings corresponding to the current status of each type of data stored in the internal library, and run notebooks showing the output results of test runs. The external library also contains archives documents — older versions of the current-status listings to be used for historical purposes and as backups in case of loss of current documents.

The Development Support Library serves as the single location for the official version of the program system being developed. It virtually eliminates the retention of private versions of modules by individual programmers, and it makes the current system completely visible and open to inspection by all project members. All submissions of new code, changes in existing code, requests for test runs, and so on, are submitted through the technical librarian, someone specially trained for the job. This librarian is the interface between the programmer and the computer; he enters all new inputs into the system, and distributes all new outputs to the appropriate notebooks and binders. The technical librarian handles a good many clerical chores, thus releasing the programmers from those responsibilities.

A given Development Support Library may contain more than one program system at a time because:

- There may be versions of a system at different levels of completion at any one time, especially on larger projects (see Chapter 8).

- The library may serve a larger community than just your project. There is no reason why a number of projects may not make use of the same library facility. In this case, more than one technical librarian may be needed.

Every set of data, whether program code, control code, or test data, is uniquely identified within the library. Unique identifiers are used to separate different versions of a program from one another and entirely different projects from one another.

Of course, it's important that the technical librarian be well trained and capable, for the job is an important one. It's important, too, that he be thick-skinned and not easily bribed. Programmers should not be allowed to skirt the library procedures; otherwise, the library immediately loses its value as a vital project control point. Programmers are infamous for putting in those little last-minute changes (see Fig. 4.5). *There are no little changes.* Each change is

Figure 4.5. Just one more little change[4]

[4] Reprinted by permission from *Programming Project Management Guide,* © 1970 by International Business Machines Corporation.

potential dynamite, especially if you're nearing system or acceptance test. Guard against those midnight patches by making internal library storage virtually inaccessible. Your programmers may be irked, but that's better than having an acceptance test blow up in your face while the customer is looking on.

THE MANAGER'S JOB

The manager's job is the promotion of excellence. Simply getting a task done, meeting deadlines, living within budgets, rewarding workers fairly, pleasing the customer, maintaining personal and company integrity, etc.—these are essential, but not enough. The manager should always be looking for ways to provide an excellent product and at the same time ensure the personal satisfaction and career growth of his people. Those things go hand-in-hand; an excellent product will enhance the careers of its makers, and growing and satisfied people will produce a better product.

There are a great many differing and sometimes conflicting views on how to go about managing. Townsend [29] describes the manager as the one who "carries water for his people so they can get on with the job." I know many excellent managers who agree with this view. (I also know some who hold the opposite, a sort of Ptolemaic view, that the universe exists to serve *them*!)

"Carrying the water" is important, but there's more. To be really effective, a manager must be respected, and to be respected he must lead. That doesn't mean charging San Juan Hill with drawn saber. It means knowing enough and knowing how to find and use competent technical advice to be able to *set technical direction* for the organization. A tough job, but necessary to the pursuit of excellence.

The following sections describe the functions of a manager in a programming organization. In many ways these functions are the same for a first-level manager as they are for an upper-level manager. Significant differences between the first-level and the upper-level management job are summarized in the last section.

Technical Leadership

The manager need not be the best technical person in the organization in order to establish its technical direction. What he does need, besides the obvious attributes, is an intense desire for his people to be in tune with the business' technology and for the managers to understand the latest management methods.

In the programming business there has been an increasing tendency, and a healthy one, to bind more closely together management and programming techniques. Programming management has perhaps become somewhat more specialized. One theory of management says that a good manager can handle either a meat market or a computer project equally well, and no doubt that's true for a gifted handful of individuals. For many others, though, the product would always be hamburger.

Throughout this book I've mentioned programming developments such as structured programming, top-down development, HIPO charts, structured walk-throughs, code inspections, and Development Support Libraries. These are all tools conceived by computer scientists, programmers, managers — people who are interested in improving the quality of the programming process and product. What strikes me about all these methodologies is that they are *both* technical tools and management tools. In every case they assist technical people in the execution of their jobs, all the way from analysis through designing, coding, and testing their products. But at the same time these techniques are helping technical leaders and managers to control the development process. What I think this says to managers is:

1. The traditional manager's manual is not enough; get to know thoroughly these technical/managerial tools and use them to communicate with your technical people. With HIPO charts showing functional design in a top-down manner, there is no reason why the project manager should not understand them.[5] With many detailed designs expressed in combinations of HIPO and pseudo code, there is no excuse for a first-level manager not to understand what the programmers are doing. Given the very important focus and control point offered by a Development Support Library, there is much more opportunity for anyone on the project to understand system status.

2. Make sure that you always allow time and money in your budget — insist on it — for all project members to continue their career educations. Don't simply send managers to management classes and technical people to technical classes; send

[5] In an unpublished 1976 paper, "Human Productivity in Software Development." Harlan Mills, one of the top leaders in the development of new programming and management methods, says: "If management doesn't review design (and suggest valid improvements now and then) and doesn't read code (and recognize excellence), programmers are not likely to care either."

some of each to the other. And don't rely on the traditional classes offered by your company or by a vendor or user; set up your own classes for your project. Suppose most of your people are unfamiliar with top-down design or structured code or HIPO or whatever; organize classes and seminars for them. Encourage them to take the time to learn about their business without having to feel guilty because they're not "producing."

Where technical leadership is concerned, I understand the tendency to feel no longer competent to dig into technical matters once you become a manager. But the tools are there for you to understand and contribute if you will only (1) learn the tools, and (2) make sure your technical people understand that you want to understand and you expect them to communicate with you in language you can understand.

Planning and Controlling

These activities are at the core of every management job. Planning means laying out what you want to happen; controlling means making sure it does happen. Planning and controlling are what this entire book is about.

Communicating

The problem most people have in communicating is not how well they speak, but how well they *listen*. One manager I know is an especially poor listener. Anyone going into his office with a problem can be absolutely guaranteed that within minutes the conversation will turn to the *manager's* problems.

Some people are poor at oral communication but compensate for it by writing things down. After a meeting, for example, this type of person jots down what he thinks was said or what decisions were reached at the meeting. That's good technique. There are meetings every day in any organization from which people come away with completely different impressions of what was said or decided.

A manager ought to communicate his own management philosophy to the people working with him. It's a difficult assignment, but people must know. I don't suggest that you call a meeting to make a speech entitled "My Management Philosophy," but you can call frequent project meetings and take advantage of any reasonable opening to talk about how you see things. Practically anything is fair game. Talk about how you expect to organize, what kinds of responsibility you expect people to assume, how much latitude an individual has, what you think about taking time to read periodicals and newspapers at work, your views on tardiness, what political problems you foresee for the project, and so on. If you can casually discuss these topics, you'll let people know the general direction of your thinking, and you'll have a group of people who better understand the job. But *don't forget to listen.* Don't become so spellbound by your own words that you don't solicit and listen to opposing viewpoints from your people. If the people at your project meetings eventually speak up and *question* your remarks and your way of handling things, you've succeeded. You've replaced monolog with dialog. *Listen* and follow up with brisk action.

A final point on communicating: establish basic definitions for your project and *insist* that they be used consistently. Consider this conversation that I overheard:

"Where does your job stand, Dick?"

"Pretty good. I think we're in system test."

"Oh, you mean integration?"

"Yeah, I guess so . . . "

How can people work together on a project unless there are some basic agreements about who's doing what? Dick "thinks" he's in "system test," whatever that means, but he readily substitutes the word "integration." No doubt, he would agree to many other substitutions so that people will leave him alone and he can return to whatever it is he's doing.

Carrying the Water

Whatever the product you are building, it's *your people* who put it together. Part of your job is to provide them with the environment and the tools they need to perform. You must maximize their chances of success.

One thing you can do is set up the best physical facilities you can afford. Maybe programmers don't need carpeted offices, but they need quiet and privacy. The programming process can tolerate neither a noisy factory environment nor constant interruptions.

If we could perhaps hang a dollar sign on each distraction or disruption a programmer experiences in the course of a day, we would quickly invest in some remedies. Consider the effect of interrupting a programmer in the middle of a complex piece of code. Later he not only has to backtrack to pick up the thread of what he was doing, but he may easily forget some part of what he originally had in mind. Result: a bug. The bug leads to a loss of his own time during module test; it consumes extra computer time; it may show up during higher-level tests when it will cause a disproportionate loss of people time and computer time.

Another area in which you can help the entire programming process is in providing the best possible test environment. You can raise hell with the computer center to provide adequate and *predictable* computer services. You can arrange for courier service and pickup and drop areas for test runs. You can throw a tantrum when anyone suggests splitting your programmers in two so that some of them can use third-shift computer time. Communication is tough enough without adding that horror.

And speaking of communication, try your best to establish an environment in which people speak out and tell you when things are not right. One way to do this is to be on the alert for the first comment that sounds like a valid complaint or criticism, pounce on it, fix whatever was being criticized, and make sure that everyone knows you acted positively because of someone's criticism. Conversely, if you turn off the first criticism, you'll never hear another, constructive or otherwise. Some time ago I attended a project meeting in which the boss discussed status, levied a few new ground rules, asked for questions, and adjourned the meeting when there were no questions. Immediately afterward, a small knot of programmers gathered near my office and hanged management *in absentia.* I listened in and then asked the most vocal member of the group why he hadn't spoken up in the meeting. He answered that management never listens, anyway, so why bother. How many times this happens every day is anybody's guess, but there's only one person who can prevent it: you, the manager. You set the tone.

The manager should also act as a buffer by taking steps to get needed information to his people and to screen the trivia. Any large organization is plagued by too much paper going to too many of the wrong people. This often happens because a manager bucks everything on to his other people with a "read and pass on" note. Either he is afraid to withhold information that staff members may need or he is afraid to miss something that one of them may pick up. No matter how safe it may make you feel, you simply cannot have everyone read everything.

Finally, to emphasize what I've discussed earlier, be sure that in your project planning specific thought is given to search out the most appropriate tools for both management and programming. It takes enlightened management to *encourage* people to read the literature, snoop around, and do the digging required to come up with new tools and new ways of doing a job.

Assigning the Work

If this book were printed in color, I'd have this section done in blazing red. Of all the things I've seen done badly, assigning the work is at the top of the list. I once witnessed a large proposal effort whose objective was to win a huge programming job under contract to the federal government. The proposal itself involved more than fifty people. *No one* was appointed proposal manager. People were loosely assigned to jobs. Some areas of work were covered by three or four people each of whom thought that he or she alone should be doing that job. Other areas were not covered at all. The manager who had the power to correct all this had a reputation for not making specific assignments. He waited, often in vain, for a hero to step forth and volunteer. Things just don't work that way. The person in a position to direct *must* direct.

The solution is so simple. First, assign a specific person for any job. The idea that a busy executive can be acting manager of a major project in his spare time is ridiculous; that's what happened on the proposal mentioned above. Better to appoint a slightly less qualified person to the job full time than to assign the job to an acting manager who can't devote enough time to do the job justice.

Now suppose that you have been assigned as manager of a project or proposal effort. You must first gain an understanding of the job. *Then* make an attempt at breaking up the job and assigning pieces of it to individuals. But this is not enough. You must write down a description of each person's job. I can't say it strongly enough. *Write it down!* Then give a copy of *all* assignments to everyone. The first thing that will happen is that half your crew will come storming in to complain that someone else's job assignment bites into their territory. If you're lucky, someone will come in and point out that *nobody's* assignment covers area X. After you've had a couple days of complaints, and people have chewed on the assignments enough, set up a meeting to talk over the problems that have been brought to you. Then rewrite the assignments, pass them out again, and wait for the second round of blasts. It may take a couple of repetitions, and some of the meetings may be uncomfortable, but soon you'll have job descriptions that *don't* overlap and *do* cover what needs to be done.

An alternate approach is to assign work by topic only, and let each one write his own work description. Then you alter them in whatever way you see fit, and pass them out. It doesn't matter which approach you take, as long as all tasks are fully covered and everyone knows exactly what his job is and what others' jobs are.

Working Hours

If you're relatively new to the computer programming business, perhaps you have not yet taken part in panic projects where everything was late and management had to resort to that ultimate remedy: scheduled overtime.

I doubt that there is a much worse waste of resources than this. There is a natural temptation to think that by working a given set of people 25% more hours a week, 25% more work will get done; some managers even think that crash overtime efforts help to bring the troops together and that a strong feeling of camaraderie develops — something like having a buddy in the foxhole with you. But experience proves otherwise.

First, 25% more hours can easily produce 10% less work, or at least less usable work. Given more hours to work each day for an extended period of weeks or months, most people will simply settle into a new routine, pacing themselves more slowly. Their work may get sloppier.

The first week, of course, some extra work may indeed get done, and perhaps even the second and the third, but after that it may be a losing effort. People unconsciously slow their efforts to fill the scheduled time. And even extra work accomplished during that first week or two will not be nearly in proportion to its cost — either the dollar cost or the cost in morale as private and family lives are inevitably intruded upon. And as for that feeling of camaraderie, it soon evolves into negativism: damn the customer for insisting on that delivery deadline; damn management for agreeing to it; damn the computer time; damn everything!

Note that we're discussing *scheduled* overtime. It simply does not work well. The only real chance for overtime to work well is when it's done *voluntarily* and over short time spans. Mills says this about overtime:

> It is almost impossible to imagine a situation where directed overtime would not reduce total productivity. If the motivation is not present

for voluntary overtime to increase productivity, it surely will not be generated by involuntary overtime. . . . If high motivation brings voluntary (unpaid) overtime, increased productivity may result in the short run — a few weeks, say. But in the long run, even a voluntary overtime activity may be counterproductive. Enthusiasm may wear off, and be replaced by resentment at being expected to put in overtime by precedent, if not by direction. Overtime may become a habit and an excuse for not working smarter [41] .

There is something else to consider about working hours. Various companies have experimented with the idea of letting employees set their own hours. Generally, the total time to be worked each day is set, but starting and ending times are allowed to float. This can be further liberalized by setting a number of hours for, say, an entire week, and leaving the specific days or hours up to the individual. Carried a step further, hours might be eliminated as a measure of work or worth; the means of measurement or control might be that the employee complete a given task by some predetermined date!

Perhaps those latter notions are too liberal for now, but the idea of the floating work*day* is not. It's been tried and it's been shown it can work. It has the obvious advantage of catering to the individual needs and inclinations and body clocks of each employee, which should lead to improved satisfaction with one's job. There are also obvious disadvantages — for example, how can you call a department meeting when you never know who will be around at any given hour? And how about the frustrations of programmer A who needs to talk to programmer B, but A's chosen hours are early in the day and B's are late?

An obvious way to experiment with the set-your-own-hours idea is to start small, see how well it works, and adjust as you go along. Begin by limiting the range over which the individuals' hours might float. Set aside a part of each day, say 1:00 P.M. to 4:00 P.M., when everyone is expected to be on the job. That will allow some to work from 7:00 A.M. to 4:00 P.M., others from 1:00 P.M. to 9:00 P.M., still others from 10:00 A.M. to 7:00 P.M. Sound like a management headache? All right then, back to your cave!

Adding More People

Just as resorting to overtime is generally wasteful, neither is it helpful as a rule to load the project with more people to try to bail out of problems which are the result of poor planning in the first place.

Beware of holding to impossible deadlines in the mistaken belief that what you lack in calendar time you can make up with bodies. It just does not work. Brooks [37] claims to be oversimplifying outrageously when he postulates Brooks' Law: *Adding manpower to a late software project makes it later.* But having witnessed and participated in exactly such ill-fated rescue activities, I think his law makes terribly good sense. "The bearing of a child," says Brooks, "takes nine months, no matter how many women are assigned."

There are two reasonable alternatives to adding more people when the project falls behind schedule:

1. Reschedule. This, of course, will make the customer scream; and that will make your management scream.

2. Arrange to deliver interim, incomplete versions of your system. If the first delivery can be made at the time you were supposed to deliver the final product, that timing should help; only the final version, then, need be rescheduled.

If you become involved in rescheduling and delivering interim versions of the system, be as sure as you can that this time you can make the deliveries as promised. There will be a terribly compelling urge to deliver as soon as possible, and it's probable that you'll offer new dates that are again too optimistic. Best to make your stand now, admit to any bad planning or execution you've been responsible for so far, but make sure you don't repeat those mistakes. Screaming customers are a nightmare, as are screaming bosses. Don't let their screams wear you down when you feel you're right; otherwise, you'll hear them scream again in a few months.

Reporting Technical Status

Anyone who is doing a job for anyone else must somehow communicate how things are going. Usually, there is a need for both written reports and oral reviews. Let's consider each in turn.

Written reports. Reporting the status of anything presupposes that there is some baseline plan to report against. It is of little use to report that program module ABC has been tested if there never was a plan showing when ABC *should* have been tested. Therefore, the first requirement for effective status reporting is that there must be a plan and milestones against which to measure progress (see Chapter 2).

A second consideration is that all reports should be tailored to fit the management level for which they are intended. They should be tailored both in terms of content and frequency. A reasonable scheme for your project might work like this: Individuals, for example, programmers, report biweekly to their first-level managers on the status of all tasks, or work packages, to which they have been assigned. The first-level manager, after receiving inputs from his people, reports to the second-level manager the status of *selected* tasks; that is, he reports on those tasks shown as milestones on his work assignment bar chart. A first-level manager responsible for, say, fifteen tasks, might report to a second-level manager only four or five. In turn, the second-level manager reports to you the status of milestone tasks on his charts. Effectively, then, what you receive is a net summation of all the individual pieces of work on the project. Rather than pass on all possible status data, each manager acts as a filter and lets through only that which is important. In turn, you pass on a condensed report to your management and to the customer (see Fig. 4.6). All the reports in this chain should follow similar, compatible formats. That way, if you occasionally call for more data from a manager, he can give you the more detailed reports gotten from his subordinates, and the detailed reports will make sense to you.

In the section of a report in which you discuss problems, state the problems, but make them appropriate to the level of the reader. Don't whine to a high mucky-muck manager about your problem in getting a new file cabinet. If you can't solve that one, the manager is going to wonder about you just a little. State your problems according to their priorities; that is, make sure the reader of the report knows which problems you consider most important. Always try to indicate potential solutions and the status of attempts at finding solutions. Give the reader the warm feeling that you're working on the problem (if you are). Earlier I emphasized laying out all the work on the project in discrete chunks. Report on those discrete chunks in your status reports. Don't let anyone get by with qualitative mealy-mouthing or meaningless "percent complete" reports. Insist that your people report to you in quantitative terms. I recall one project many years ago in which we reported partly by filling in a bar chart. When a bar became entirely black, that job was theoretically done. Unfortunately, we ran out of bars before the job was finished. We found that filling in the bars told us nothing. They made depressing wall decorations in a status-control room.

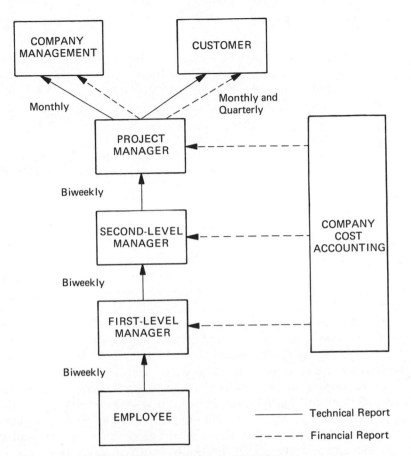

Figure 4.6. Status reporting

Oral reviews. These were discussed in Chapter 3. Here, however, I'd like to emphasize the usefulness of oral reviews. They are a great excuse for getting everyone together, whether or not they succeed in exposing any hidden problems. Project reviews help give people a sense of belonging to something besides their two-by-four cubicles. *They help people to understand the part their work plays in the total job.* They provide a break from routine. And, of course, they provide a forum for uncovering problems and broaching better solutions. You can help your project immensely if you set up these reviews in order to give people an opportunity to be heard. You might even come to be looked upon as a human being rather than that recluse who sits in the corner office with the door closed.

Reporting Financial Status

Financial reports are often generated by some cost-accounting function separate from the management of the project. These reports may be sent only to you, the project manager, or to each of your subordinate managers. Whatever the case, you should insure during planning that the tasks, or work packages, to be used as the basis for financial reporting are the same tasks used for technical reporting. You should always be able to equate technical and financial reports without need for a massive conversion exercise to find out how the two reports relate.

Training

Every manager has responsibility for training his people, totally apart from any training that must be done under the contract. The manager must seek to raise the level of competence and understanding of every individual in the organization. Otherwise, the organization stagnates. When times are tough and an organization's overhead costs must be trimmed, education is one of the first expenses cut. It's considered a luxury. Classes are cancelled because they add to overhead, and yet the same people who would have attended those classes now sit around, still charging their time to some form of overhead, doing little or nothing. I know that there are many reasons for this, mostly having to do with internal company bookkeeping. But books be damned! Get those idle people into education programs and let the bookkeepers worry about the books. (Of course, if you work for a company that gets rid of people as soon as they become idle, the argument is academic.)

There are several kinds of training a manager ought to provide, and there are a number of ways of providing it.

Let's start with your technical people, for example, the programmers. They should be trained in, or at least exposed to, programming languages and computers *other than* those of concern on their current projects. How else will they be able to grow? How can they offer you alternative technical solutions if all they know is machine x and language y? These people should be given the time and the encouragement to attend formal classes, subscribe to and read technical literature, and hobnob with their counterparts on other projects. The latter is often hard for a manager to swallow. It's like encouraging coffee breaks. But what a payoff! What so often results from a bull session is either a new technical idea or a pitfall to avoid.

140

Your newer programmers need special attention until you have a feel for the competence of each. Managers, especially green managers, often tend to accept their new recruits as experienced, professional people without demanding any proof. I could write a whole chapter on incidents involving programmers fresh out of school (and a few who were more experienced and should have known better). For example, consider Greg whose way of unit testing a certain math routine was quietly to increase a hidden counter (posing as a "constant" in his program) by "1" until the answer to a given test case came out right! Of course, the program never worked for any input values except those he specifically included in his test cases. And there was Bill, who didn't trust index registers and never used them. Or Ned, who, instead of using a single Clear-and-Add instruction, always put two identical Clear-and-Adds in a row in case the first one didn't work. Luckily, he trusted most of the other instructions. Another winner was Don whose solution to a problem was always to branch around the offending code. "It was just a *little* branch," he would say.

How do you recognize Greg, Bill, Ned and Don and set them straight? By making code walk-throughs and code reading routine procedures for every programmer on the project. The work of Mills and others has shown this approach to be extremely valuable, both as a quality control technique and as a training mechanism.

An important kind of training for all your people (and you) is *rotation* through jobs other than their normal ones. This can often be done without an enormous investment in time, and the payoff is handsome. Programmers who bitch about the machine room operations can learn plenty and contribute plenty just by becoming computer operators for a few days; operators will become better operators by taking some basic programming courses; programmers will become better documenters (and designers) if they spend some time in maintaining other people's programs.

Rotation, or cross-training, is helpful to your nontechnical people, too. How about a basic course in the fundamentals of system analysis, design, and programming for your secretaries and typists. They would enjoy knowing what all those scribbles are about, and would do a better job of transcribing them. There is no one on the project who would not benefit from at least some exposure to what goes on outside his own job, and this will in turn benefit the project.

A word of caution: Federal and some state labor laws severely restrict the types and duration of rotations you may legally use. You may not, for example, freely interchange "professional" and "clerical" people. Ask your company's lawyers what's allowable in your area. (Don't ask them if you can do it; it's easy to say no. Tell them you're going to, and ask how to do it legally.)

Then there are your managers. They need day-to-day assistance from you; they also need to attend management classes and seminars. They need technical updating classes to help stave off obsolescence. The managers working for you need to see in you a good example of how to manage. If you plan your activity poorly (and rely on excessive overtime to get your own work done), you're providing, by example, training in sloppy management.

Perhaps most important of all — and I've said this before — you must bring together the entire project often enough to update everyone on status and plans. It's impossible to overstate the benefits the project will receive from simply having everyone understand what is going on and where each fits in.

Appraising and Counseling

As manager you have an enormous amount of influence on the lives of your people. How well you pay a person is important, of course, but just as important is your ability to help each person on your project to find a fulfilling job. Many things about the project may be bad, but if you can just carve out a piece of work that appeals to an individual and is within his capabilities, other problems fade. Nietzsche said, "He who has a *why* to live for can bear almost any *how*."

You and your employees must agree on a suitable task and a schedule for doing it. Again, the simple act of writing down a description of people's assignments and getting their agreement to it can be extremely helpful. Often you can let people set their own schedules. You'll be surprised how hard they will work to meet a deadline they themselves fixed.

When one of your people goes off course or does a bad job, you've got to let him know it the best way you can. This can be so difficult that some managers avoid doing it until forced to. By then things are usually at crisis stage. A way of avoiding big problems is to subdivide the job sufficiently and have enough checkpoints so that missing one is a signal, not a catastrophe.

The kind of manager I've always had difficulty in understanding is the one who tells you what you've done wrong but not what you've done right. I remember one who was good at pointing out my mistakes, but when I finally asked him one day whether there was anything I had done for him with which he was satisfied, he was astonished. *Of course* he was satisfied. Didn't I realize that anything he didn't criticize was, by definition, okay? This man, who was a fine manager in most respects, simply did not understand that people *need* a good word now and then, that some people, in the absence of any good news, tend to fear the worst.

Any manager's success should be gauged by how well he encourages growth and by how fairly hard work is rewarded and incompetence dealt with. A good manager will not hesitate to promote a subordinate to the manager's own level. A good manager will not selfishly hide a key employee within the organization; instead, the manager will promote the employee and risk losing him or her to some other group. And a good manager will never transfer a "problem child" to someone else without full warning.

Sanity Maintenance

I've seen many managers get into tons of trouble because they could not say *no*. The word is negative, after all, and no eager young manager wants to sound negative. Anything the boss (or the customer) wants must be done. Since all the books on "positive thinking" and "thinking big" say you can do anything, you must strike the word "no" from your vocabulary. Rubbish! There are many things that are impossible and many more that are unreasonable. The *real* positive thinker is the person who can sort things out and distinguish between the reasonable and the unreasonable. There have been countless disasters in the programming business because someone allowed himself to be pressured into committing his efforts to something he really felt was impossible. I have participated in and observed many situations in which such pressure has been applied. Sometimes it's of the gentle variety; your manager is in a tough position and needs a certain commitment from you in order to save himself. Sometimes the pressure is applied by erosion; you're asked to give in a little at a time, in easy installments, and when you finally realize what you've done, it's too late. Other times you are fast-talked and lulled into playing RAM (Repeat After Me); the manager tells you what he wants to hear and your only job is to say it. And in still other cases, strong-arm methods are applied; you are made to feel your future promotions or your very job are in jeopardy.

There are many situations in which these tactics are applied. Perhaps what is at issue is an estimate that you have submitted; it's too high for the boss to swallow. Or maybe you're being asked to accept some added work you don't feel you can handle. I'll never forget the situation my boss found himself in some time ago. He sat behind a desk heaped high with papers; his shirt was rumpled, his tie askew, his whole appearance dishevelled. He looked numb. His manager and the customer had heaped on him so many demands that he was bewildered. He couldn't even make a start. (I suggested he start by setting fire to his desk, but he didn't think that was funny.) He had simply gotten overcommitted. He was incapable of saying "no." It happened, not entirely by coincidence, that he had a good many personnel problems at the time, all demanding his attention.

IBM's Bill Weimer has been responsible for many innovative training courses for both management and technical people. In deciding on the approach and content of one set of courses, he said, ". . . we found that technical people, in general, were actually very good at estimating project requirements and schedules. The problem they had was defending their decisions; they needed to learn how to hold their ground."

Charles P. Lecht has this to say about refusing the impossible:

> Equally responsible for the initiation of a project with predefined failure . . . is management that insists upon having fixed commitments from programming personnel prior to the latter's understanding what the commitments are for. Too frequently management does not realize that in asking the staff for the "impossible," the staff will feel the obligation to respond out of respect, fear, or misguided loyalty. Saying "no" to the boss frequently requires courage, political and psychological wisdom, and business maturity that comes with much experience [31].

There is another way to help maintain balance in the hectic business of programming management. Force yourself periodically (perhaps once a day) to take a few steps back and look at the total job, not the details. Simplify. Try to get things in perspective. Get away from the job physically—no phone, no in-basket. List all the things that you have to do and then decide which items on the list are *really* important. If there's more there than you can do, pass some of it on to someone else. Look for those items that you could cross off the list and never do (there are *always* some of these). If you take frequent enough looks, you'll begin to look at the job more rationally. You'll have a constant awareness of how much you have to do, and, therefore, how much more you can take on.

In assigning priorities to the tasks you have to do, the "people problems" should come first. Don't let your people feel that they come second to anything. If you lose their loyalty and respect, you're dead.

First-Level vs. Upper-Level Management

In the preceding discussion I haven't made much distinction between the various levels of management. The job is essentially the same, regardless of level. What really varies is the ratio of technical to non-technical involvement. This ratio decreases as you go up in the management chain. A first-level manager is normally very directly involved in the technical work his people are doing. A second-level manager's technical involvement is broader; this position requires more time than that of the first-level manager on financial matters, proposals, planning, personnel matters, and the like. And so it goes until at some level the manager is concerned much more with general business decisions than with detailed technical decisions.

A difficult problem arises from all this: How does the upper-level manager have any feel for what's going on technically? How does the manager fight technical obsolescence and have any confidence that things are going well?

There are some partial answers to these questions. First, a manager should devote a significant portion of time to technical updating by reading specifications and hearing briefings by his subordinates. *But* he must resist the urge to bit-fiddle and leave detailed technical work to those best qualified to do it. One third-level manager I know couldn't resist the urge to get into the programmers' code. While he was messing with bits, his project fell apart and was eventually cancelled.

Second, the manager should set up technical checks and balances to help assure that the technical work is getting done properly. One such check is the separate analysis and design organization discussed earlier in this chapter. Another is the separate test group also described. And still another is the extensive use of structured walk-throughs or inspections to provide for detailed scrutiny of all the items developed on the project.

A third way to keep afloat technically is to return periodically to technical work. In some organizations switching between management and technical jobs is discouraged, but if you can accomplish it, it can do wonders for your technical competence and greatly enhance your confidence in being able to manage the next job.

Finally, the manager must read the literature in his field and attend classes whenever possible. Often this will have to be done on one's own time.

Chapter 5

The System Test Phase

The system test phase is the phase toughest to sell. Both managers and programmers resist it, and yet it's as critical as any period on the project. Its main objective is to subject the programmers' products to a thorough set of tests neither designed nor executed by the programmers and run in as nearly a live environment as possible with a minimum of simulation. A second objective is to begin training the customer to be ready to take over the new system.

SYSTEM TESTING

One reason managers sometimes resist system test is that they consider it a delay en route to acceptance and delivery of the product, but they inevitably learn that system testing will not be denied. The bugs not found because system test is skipped will show up later, either during acceptance testing or after the programs have been accepted and made operational. The cost of a problem found that late is very high; it is measured in terms of customer dissatisfaction or disgust, lost opportunities for follow-on work, a tarnished reputation, and a patched-up product, as well as manpower, time, and money.

Be ready for system testing when the programmers deliver their product. Have test specifications written, computer time roughly scheduled, library facilities set up, and people ready.

System Test Specification

Test specification layouts are included in the Documentation Plan in Part II. A test specification describes the testing objectives and approach. It also contains a requirements coverage matrix showing every requirement the program system is to meet versus specific, numbered test cases designed to validate that those requirements have been met. This matrix is important; for any given system requirement, or function, it should be easy to locate in this matrix all relevant test cases. If you have trouble writing this matrix, it may signal a fuzzy set of tests.

How many test cases are needed? This is entirely up to you, but the idea is to make one test case cover a specific functional area—for example, "startup," "input message error processing," "single target detection," "target tracking," "tax computation," "single matrix conversion." The names of the functions you choose are irrelevant. Choose chunks of function big enough to be meaningful to a user, small enough that test results may be easily assimilated and understood. As a wild guess, any program system big enough to employ your forty-member group for over twelve months would probably require a set of at least forty test cases. It's impossible to offer any more solid guideline without considering the specific system being tested.

As outlined in Part II, each test case consists of a script, data, and checklists. A *script* is a set of step-by-step instructions intended to lead the test personnel almost mechanically through the tests. The script lists all actions required of human operators at each piece of equipment involved in the test. It not only tells the testers what to do and when to do it but also what to look for and what to write down for later analysis. The assumption must be made that a tester understands the background and objectives of each test, so that very little explanatory information need be included in the script. A sample page from a script is shown in Figure 5.1 Note that the right-hand portion of the page is left blank for jotting down notes during the test.

The data portion of a test case includes simulated input data, live input data, and predicted output data. *Simulated* input data are data prepared beforehand for the purpose of exercising the system during a given test. For example, if your system is a payroll processing system, these inputs may include employee hours worked, tax information, bond deductions, and the like.

Live inputs are those that cannot conveniently be prepared ahead

PROJECT XYZ TEST SCRIPT	
Test Case No. __M 14__	Page _6_ of _9_

PROCEDURES	NOTES
CONSOLE #4: 1–When ATT lights, enter date in five digits, mmddy 2–Depress ACCEPT button 3–Compare displayed date to what you entered 4–If wrong, so note, depress ATT button and repeat steps 1–3 5– . . . 6– . . . 7–Compare console status indicators to checklist number M14-1 8– . . . INPUT STATION #1: 1–When ATT lights, depress DATA button 2–Load next card pack into reader 3– . . . 4– . . . 5– . . .	

Figure 5.1. Sample page, system test script

of time, such as telemetry data from a satellite. This kind of input provides advantages that are difficult to get from prepared, simulated input data, including randomness and the likelihood of a certain amount of "garbage" that your system will have to handle properly.

Predicted outputs are written forecasts of the exact data that should result from a given test case, where such forecasting is possible. If results are determined in advance, it is only necessary to compare actual with predicted test outputs in order to determine the effectiveness of the test. Predicting outputs in advance offers advantages other than simplifying posttest analysis. It can save calendar time because the prediction can be done in parallel with other activities, before the actual tests are run. Also, it can be more accurate than on-the-spot posttest analysis because the latter often gives rise to hasty decisions (Oh, it looks all right!).

PROJECT XYZ TEST CHECKLIST			
Test Case No. __M14__ Checklist No. __M14-2__ Page _1_ of _3_			
No.	Item	Yes	No
1-0	DISPLAY CONSOLES		
1-1	Were all displays easy to read?		
1-2	Were all displayed instructions clear and unambiguous?		
1-3	Were all displayed messages complete?		
1-4	Were all displayed data arranged well?		
1-5	. . .		
1-6	. . .		
2-0	OPERATING ENVIRONMENT		
2-1	Was there sufficient light for easy operation of all controls?		
2-2	Is the equipment arranged in the best manner for ease of operation?		
2-3	. . .		
2-4	. . .		

Figure 5.2. Partial system test checklist

The final portion of a test case is a set of checklists prepared in advance to help during posttest analysis. Checklists are powerful analysis aids when they are thoughtfully constructed. An example of a partial checklist is shown in Figure 5.2.

Each test case should be self-contained, independent of all the others. Within each test there should be built-in restart points, convenient places for resuming in the event of unexpected aborts during the test.

Every test should be planned so that in posttest analysis it can be clearly shown what the inputs were, what the results were predicted to be, and what the results actually were.

The Testers

Those who plan, execute, and analyze the tests belong to the Test Group shown in Figure 4.3. These people must be technically competent and analytically inclined. They must thoroughly understand the customer and the Problem Specification. Some of the group should have participated in the original problem analysis. At least one member of the group should be a user.

Try to instill an air of friendly (but not too friendly) competition between the testers and the programmers. The system testers are out to unearth problems. If they find none, either they are bums, your programmers are heroes, or your system was extremely simple to build. You should *expect* problems. Some of them may be due to errors, but many will be matters of interpretation of the Problem Specification or problems in ease of use of the system. Some in the latter category may be the result of faulty user documents rather than programming bugs. *Any* problem is fair game. The system testers must "think customer" and constantly appraise the system from the customer's point of view.

Don't choose as system testers people who are bland, easily intimidated, or technically dull. These people should be demonic in their attempts to make the system fail. A system failure is their success. They must be encouraged to poke into all the dark corners of the system. *Never* suggest to them that they might go easy in a particular area; remember, what they don't find, the customer eventually will.

Timing

No test phase should begin until test entry criteria have been met. Specific entry criteria will vary, depending on the product being tested, but generally they include the following:

- The product to be tested (program or document) must be considered complete by its developers; any exceptions must have explicit management approval.

- The written test specification for that product must be finished, approved, and ready for execution.

- All supporting test data must be ready.

- Both the developers and the testing people must be present, or on call.

- Computer time, if needed, must be scheduled.

- Any special resources (for example, remote equipment, temporary living facilities at a remote site, transportation) must be ready.

One project I know of did plan for a system test phase, which was admirable. But as time went by and deadlines were missed, management decided something had to be done in parallel with something else in order to speed things up. So system test was done (no, *attempted*) in parallel with the late months of the Programming Phase. To make matters worse, this project attempted to do even more in parallel by conducting system test in several locations at once. To top it off, some of the locations were halfway around the world! The result was chaos. Within a few days, so many bugs had been found that many modules found themselves back in module test. The coordination problem among all the sites was a monster. Imagine half a dozen versions of a system consisting of hundreds of modules being debugged at half a dozen separate sites! The people on this project were extremely able and competent, but they were frantically looking for a way out of a problem which had arisen at birth: at the outset the calendar time scheduled for the project was totally inadequate, and everyone knew it. The misery was compounded when very early in the project it was changed from a single-customer to a multiple-customer job, with no substantive change in the work scope, funding, or anything else. When political or economic pressures mount, the ablest of men throw out everything they know about good management. This buys them some time for a breather, but there's *always* the reckoning later on.

We can learn some lessons about system test from past disasters. First, no amount of luck, political acumen, or holy living will allow you to skip system testing and get away with it. In a system of any complexity at all, those hot-shot programmers are going to make mistakes — and some of them will be beauts! I feel sure that you will want to find them before your customer does.

Second, you cannot do system testing completely in parallel with programming. There's nothing yet worth testing. What you *can* do, however, is very cautiously accept less than the complete system and begin test on completed *sub*systems. This only applies when your subsystems are nearly independent of one another and the interfaces between them are clean and simple.

Third, don't spread system testing geographically until you've reached the point at which the system looks clean and only needs testing against unique site conditions. These conditions may include modified static data bases, geographic location coordinates, varying input and output devices, and varying input loads. Remember that each time you introduce another copy of your system into the test environment, you've increased your control problems. Every change in one version must be reflected and tested in all other versions. Communication is a nightmare and a drain on all kinds of resources.

Conducting the Tests

System test begins when the programmers release to the Test Group their "finished" product: a program system (or subsystem if that makes sense in your case) and clean draft documentation. The Test Group manager formally accepts, signs for, and locks up the system that he receives. Test conductors are assigned for specific groups of test cases.

A test conductor is responsible for the preparation, execution, and analysis of a set of test cases. The conductor schedules the people, the computer time, physical facilities, and any other resources required for these test cases. Before a test is begun, the conductor assures that all participants and observers are on hand and that they have all required materials, such as scripts, checklists, and predicted outputs.

The conductor initiates the test. Those taking part follow their scripts precisely, noting any discrepancies or unusual conditions. The conductor makes all decisions concerning aborts or restarts unless the script already provides for these. Observers, who may be given copies of scripts, should be encouraged to jot down ideas and questions as the test proceeds. Observers may be programmers or other project members. They may also be customer representatives. If you choose to invite the customer in order to offer a preview of the system, be certain it is understood that it is a *test* of an incomplete system, not a *demonstration* of a finished product. The customer should know that problems are expected. If he gets the idea that system test is no more than a dress rehearsal for acceptance test, there will be some degree of uneasiness, or even suspicion, every time you hit a snag.

When a test or series of tests has been completed, the conductor calls together the test participants for analysis of the results. In some instances, this analysis can be completed and an assessment of success or failure made immediately. In other cases, outputs will require study and the conductor will need to call another analysis meeting. Whatever the case, the conductor is responsible for declaring a test a success or a failure (which may mean a partial success) and reporting the result to management. A simple form should be used to document the results. It should include the test case identification number, the test date, and the result. If the result was unqualified success, no elaboration is required. If there were problems, these must be detailed, and the test conductor should follow up to be sure that programmers have been assigned to track them down and correct them. The test conductor must also take the lead in deciding what further testing must be done after a fix has been made.

After a repair there are several testing options from which to choose: (1) The fix may involve a minor documentation change only, so that no retesting need be done; (2) The change may require a major overhaul in one or more program modules because the Problem Specification was misinterpreted. Here, consultation with the customer may enable you to negotiate around making any change; (3) An analysis, design, or coding change may be required which affects portions of the system already tested. You should assume that all changes have that effect. Now the test conductor, assisted by the programmers, must decide how much *regression testing* is necessary. Regression testing is retesting of previously finished portions of the system to insure that this late change does not ripple back through the system causing some seemingly unrelated problems. Regression-test decisions are tough to make. Some of the simplest changes have a way of churning up the very bowels of the system; (4) Descriptive documentation (Coding Specifications) may be in error. These descriptions must agree exactly with the programs. Insist that every module submitted for system test be cleanly assembled or compiled — *no patches.*

When a system or subsystem has passed cleanly through the final system test, the programs and their documentation are locked in the library to await acceptance demonstration.

CUSTOMER TRAINING

A secondary objective of this phase is to prepare for and, in many cases, begin training the customer. There are at least two areas requiring customer training: *using* the system and *maintaining* the system.

Using the System

Usually, you are either replacing a manual procedure with your new automated system or you are introducing the new system where there was nothing before. In either case, customer personnel must learn to operate what you're turning over to them. You should consider all the usual means of training: formal classroom sessions, seminars, on-the-job training, and computer-assisted instruction. Some training will be unique to your project; other forms may be available through your company's regular education program.

In any case, you will need to write and deliver user manuals for use both in training and in future operation of the system. Here is an opportunity to shine. Many good program systems have been delivered accompanied by poor user guides. Bad writing reflects adversely on your whole system. Often, the user information is the only tangible part of your product for the customer. He'll judge you by the kind of writing job you do. Take pains to do it well. Find people among your analysts who have facility with words and can get a point across clearly and briefly. Get this job under way early, not three days before acceptance.

Maintaining the System

Often the customer assumes the job of making future changes to the system, and therefore must understand in detail the product you are delivering. You may be required to train a nucleus of the customer's technical people who in turn will train others. Whatever the method of training used, you will need accurate and usable documentation. Two sets of descriptive documents, the Design Specification and the Coding Specifications, should completely and accurately describe your program system. In addition, you may write special troubleshooting manuals that will enable others to understand special quirks of the system or show them short cuts for probing particularly difficult areas of code.

Sometimes customer training is a huge task because of the complexity of the system, the numbers of people to be trained, or the logistics costs involved in training exercises (perhaps missiles must be launched or armed forces units deployed). In these situations, it may be wise to provide training under a separate contract, one under which you are paid for whatever amount of effort you expend. Essentially, you keep on training until the customer says "enough." If your customer is a government agency, there are appropriate kinds of contracts available, including "labor hour" and "time and material" contracts.

Chapter 6

The Acceptance Phase

The objective of the Acceptance Phase is to demonstrate to the customer that the system you are ready to deliver satisfies the contract that you both signed. Acceptance testing is called by a variety of names: "demonstration testing," "performance test," "product verification," and so on. Whatever the name, the desired outcome is written acceptance of your product by the customer.

ACCEPTANCE TESTING

Acceptance Test Specification

As in system test, acceptance testing is laid out and formalized in a document called the Acceptance Test Specification (see Part II). The test cases are constructed in the same manner as those used in system test; indeed, many or all of them can be the same as those used in system test.

The Acceptance Test Specification should be written in concert with the customer. You draft; the customer approves.[1] There is no point presenting him with your first version of an acceptance document at the end of the project. The customer just won't agree to it, and you'll be in trouble. Instead, produce this specification in stages.

---

[1] There are many exceptions to this. Often the customer prepares the acceptance documents.

First, during the Definition Phase, write the section called "Acceptance Criteria" (or "Success Criteria"). This is one of the most critical documents on any project; it states the specific conditions under which the customer will formally accept your product. Then write the remaining sections of the Acceptance Test Specification and construct all the necessary test cases. The final specification and test cases should be finished at the same time as the System Test Specification so that the two may share test cases.

Acceptance Criteria

Acceptance criteria are the conditions that your system must satisfy before the customer will formally accept the system and agree that it satisfies the contract. Writing acceptance criteria is one of the most difficult chores you'll face. Your customer will be tough about this, and should be. The one who signs an acceptance agreement knows that his job is on the line. Any chummy agreements you and the customer may have had in the past are null and void (Fig. 6.1).

Acceptance criteria *should* be settled even before a contract is signed, and sometimes this is possible. Usually, however, little more than general criteria are agreed to that early. The very least that the contract should state are the schedule for writing the final criteria and time restrictions on the customer for reviewing your drafts. The customer must agree to accept or reject your acceptance specifications within defined periods of time. Without this clause, you may use up your entire calendar time and budget and still have no agreement about acceptance terms. In setting up times for review and revision of documents, always allow for more than a single iteration. Assume that the customer will want you to make changes and allow time for a second draft and its review.

Acceptance criteria must be based on something *quantitative*, something *measurable*. Your goal should be to remove subjectivity from assessment of test results (this applies to any test). If you can include in your criteria a statement that "report ABC shall be printed within three minutes after pushbutton request," that's far better than saying, "report ABC shall be printed within a reasonable time after pushbutton request." You and your customer can time three minutes with a stopwatch, but you may never agree on what constitutes a "reasonable" time.

Acceptance criteria cover not only required performance by the system, but delivery of the system as well. When and where should copies of the system be delivered? How many copies? In what form?

Figure 6.1. Your buddy, the customer[2]

How should materials be packaged? One of the deliverables should be the set of test cases used during acceptance demonstration.

It may be helpful to consider some examples of *bad* acceptance criteria in order to understand what would constitute *good* ones. The following examples are taken from actual acceptance documents:

> The contractor will have priority in using the customer's computers for program checkout.
>
> *What priority? Highest? Second? This statement gives you nothing.*
>
> An appropriate number of messages shall be included to test the system exhaustively.

---

[2] Reprinted by permission from *Programming Project Management Guide*, © 1970 by International Business Machines Corporation.

What's appropriate? Ten messages or ten thousand? What does "exhaustively" mean?

The contractor shall, with the customer's assistance, prepare test messages to exercise all options listed in the scope of work.

How much customer assistance? Who does the analysis? Who actually types or punches the messages? This could be either a man-week job or a man-year.

The visual display of target tracking data shall take place in a timely manner consistent with the existing threat conditions.

What does that mean? Your guess is as good as mine.

The contractor shall make such changes as the customer directs within thirty days following formal acceptance demonstration.

This statement within proper context might not be bad, but it was not in proper context. It amounted to an open-ended commitment by the contractor.

The strange thing about all these goofs is that they were taken from acceptance agreements written by contractors, not by customers!

Execution

Acceptance testing is carried out in much the same way as system testing, but with the following differences: First, the customer must play an active role in acceptance testing. He must supply people to perform some or all of the manual operations. The customer will certainly figure heavily in posttest analysis and will be required, of course, to approve a test before it can be considered complete or successful. Second, the customer should insist on introducing into the system data which you have never seen or used before. Third, acceptance may be made conditional; for example, later tests at scattered geographic sites may be required in order to achieve full acceptance (see discussion of large projects in Chapter 8).

DOCUMENTATION

As acceptance testing proceeds, minor flaws may be detected in both the user documentation and the system's descriptive documentation. Corrections must be made, of course, before delivering the final documents to the customer. For this reason, final documentation should be planned and budgeted for delivery at the end of the Acceptance Phase or even later, so that corrections may be included cleanly. The alternative is to deliver documents earlier and then bear the expense and inconvenience of issuing errata sheets, which, I believe, cheapen your product.

Chapter 7

The Installation and Operation Phase

Many projects, particularly the smaller ones, end with the Acceptance Phase. The acceptance demonstrations may be conducted on the customer's equipment, and at the successful end of the demonstrations the system is already installed and operational. In other cases, however, acceptance is conditional and must be followed up by further testing at some other site, conversion from an old system to the new, and continuing maintenance and tuning. Since you may have responsibility for some or all of these tasks, I'll briefly cover them in this chapter.

SITE TESTING

Site testing must be done in the final environment in which your system is to operate — the operational site. This testing may amount to simply repeating earlier tests (acceptance tests) in the new environment. At the other extreme, site testing may be a huge job requiring a great deal of training and expense. In this latter category are the monster defense projects that require independently tested data processing, weapons, guidance, and communications subsystems to be merged and tested together at an operational site.

If your project requires site testing, you should take care to plan well for it. Write a Site Test Specification similar to the Integration, System, and Acceptance Test Specifications described earlier.

There are several areas of difference between the testing that we have discussed thus far and site testing. First, the computer equipment at the operational site may not be identical to that used during the preceding phases. There may be differences in input-output devices (for example, variations in tape speeds and densities), different versions of operating systems, different core sizes, and even different models of a family of computers which could affect the speed of execution and the instruction repertoire available.

Second, at an operational site your system may operate for the first time without simulation. Until site test time, you may have had to rely on simulation as a source of inputs to your system or as a receiver of outputs, or both. Strange things happen when simulators are replaced by the real thing, no matter how brilliantly the simulators were planned and executed.

Third, the data base that your system uses at the operational site may be different from that used previously. For example, some data may be site identifiers or geographic location coordinates. Data-base changes can drive you nuts. The tiniest adjustments must be thoroughly tested.

If your system is to be installed and tested at several sites simultaneously, make sure that the system is really ready to be sent out. The communication problems among several teams operating in the field at different locations will be difficult enough without the irritant of a buggy system that should never have been released.

CONVERSION

Generally, your system will be replacing something else, perhaps a manual operation. The customer will need to convert the operation from the old system to the new, and you may be deeply involved in the conversion. There are two kinds of conversion (and many variations of each): *parallel operation* and *immediate replacement*.

Parallel Operation

Parallel operation means that you don't throw out the old system until you're sure the new one is working. Here's what Robert Townsend has to say on the subject:

> No matter what the experts say, never, never automate a manual function without a long enough period of dual operation. When in doubt discontinue the automation. And don't stop the manual system until

the *non-experts* in the organization think that automation is working. I've never known a company seriously injured by automating too slowly but there are some classic cases of companies bankrupted by computerizing prematurely [32].

Under parallel operation, the customer has maximum flexibility. Outputs from the new system can be used immediately, with the possibility of reverting back to the old system at any time. The new system can also be phased in slowly. In this case, the customer is using parts of both systems with the eventual total replacement of the old.

Immediate Replacement

Here the old system is shut down and the new installed. Of course, this is a risky option, but there may be compelling reasons for choosing it. First, parallel operation may be virtually impossible because of limited space or other resources; second, the function performed by the system may not be so critical that a failure means disaster; third, the expense of parallel operations may be prohibitive; fourth, the new system may be a radical break with old procedures.

Cutover

Cutover is ribbon-cutting time, the point at which the old system is forever discarded and the new adopted. There are some important items concerning cutover which you and the customer should consider ahead of time.

Cutover criteria. What are the conditions under which cutover will be accomplished? When is the magic moment? Will it be done by gut feel or only after thorough inspection of system outputs?

Cutover responsibility. Who makes the decision? Normally it will be the customer, but not always. The two of you must decide this in advance.

Operating responsibility. Who actually operates the system up to the point of cutover? You or the customer, or both?

Recovery options. Almost all systems should have explicit procedures and a separate book of error messages for recovering in the event of equipment failure, human error, and so on. Recovery should have been addressed, of course, way back in the Design Phase. What's important now is that those operating the system clearly understand how to use the various recovery features.

MAINTENANCE AND TUNING

Many contracts call for the contractor to provide maintenance and tuning assistance for a specified period after delivery of the system. Maintenance means fixing problems that show up late, including bugs or documentation errors uncovered during the Acceptance Phase. Tuning is the adjustment or refinement of parameters somewhere in the system. It can only be done after the system has been observed in operation for some time. All of this work is best done under a separate "labor hours" contract under which you supply a number of people to fix whatever the customer wants fixed and the customer pays you for the expense incurred. Operating under other kinds of contracts, such as "fixed-price" contracts, can be costly because the customer may want an endless stream of "repairs" that are really new wrinkles or improvements. However you choose to operate, change control procedures must be followed. This is at least as important a function now as it was during the Programming Phase. The system is on the air, and an ill-considered change could be catastrophic.

PROJECT EVALUATION

You're finally finished with your project — almost. There's one more chore to be done. Take some time out to think about how it all went and write an evaluation report. Use it yourself as a reminder on future jobs, and give it to your management. Make use of the Project History that you've been keeping (you have, haven't you?) and include in your evaluation the following items:

1. Project overview: A few brief paragraphs describing what the problem was and how it was solved.

2. Major successes: Blow your horn. Point out major deadlines met, profitability, customer satisfaction, whatever was happy about the outcome.

3. Major problems: Come on, now, there were some, weren't there? You might place the problems in these categories: missed schedules, budget overruns, technical performance, personnel, customer relations, management support (or lack of).

4. Manpower estimates vs. actual: Get this from your Project History and present it in the form of guidelines for estimating the next job.

5. Machine time estimates vs. actual: Get this also from the Project History and tabulate the data for future use.

6. In retrospect: What you would do differently if you were to repeat this job.

Chapter 8

Special Considerations

So far we've been looking primarily at a medium-sized project, which I arbitrarily defined as forty people. Here are some thoughts about bigger and smaller projects, along with a few other ideas I felt should be treated separately.

BIG PROJECTS

First of all, do you need a big project? Do you really need a hundred, six hundred, a thousand people on a programming job? You can accomplish a great deal with a handful of *really good* people who are well managed. There's absolutely no question that your forty-person group working as a real team can accomplish more than a fractured, tough-to-manage mass of hundreds. And it may well be that even your forty people are far too many, and that this job could be handled beautifully by a Chief Programmer Team of six. It's never so obvious as on a massive, overstaffed job that 10% of the people do 90% of the work. Really think about it: do you *need* a big project?

There are some tiresome and galling arguments that lead to last-minute doubling or tripling of initial manpower estimates. One of them is this: *If you propose a significantly smaller number of people for a job than your competitors propose, your people obviously just don't understand the problem.* Another goes this way: *Since the customer expects big numbers, you'd better propose them.*

I've seen manpower estimates arbitrarily *tripled* because they didn't fall in line with the actual manpower being used by the same company on a similar project. The trouble with probing such numbers later on is that no matter how many people were put on the job they all end up apparently doing *something* to justify their presence. It's a self-fulfilling prophecy, for if you propose six hundred people to write a program, by gosh, you *use* six hundred. Each can write thirty computer instructions and two hundred status reports in order to keep busy.

Of course, some projects are legitimately big, and big projects have some problems all their own. Let's look at a few.

The Phases

In Figure I and throughout this book I've described a project in terms of six phases: Definition, Design, Programming, System Test, Acceptance, and Installation and Operation. In a big system your programs may be only one of several major subsystems, all of which must be integrated and tested together. One or more additional phases may be added to the development cycle in Figure I. The result may be something similar to Figure 8.1.

The first five phases are the same as those in Figure I, except that now the programs are clearly a *sub*system of a larger system. In parallel with the work being done on the program subsystem, other subsystems, such as hardware, are being developed, perhaps by other companies. These parallel development activities are by no means independent of one another. During the Definition Phase, and even earlier, heroic amounts of analysis and consultation are necessary in order to write specifications outlining the individual subsystems needed. This is one of the most serious hangups on any large project. In addition to the normal pushing and shoving among the separate companies vying for an attractive piece of the total job, there is

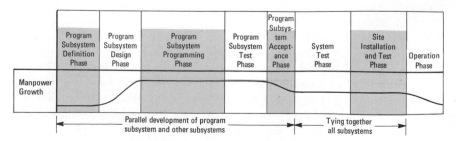

Figure 8.1. Extended development cycle

plain, honest confusion. For example, in some of the mammoth military systems the technical problems alone are staggering, let alone the questions of logistics, personnel, contracts administration, and so on. These problems are some of the reasons that projects grow so huge.

Your job will be eased considerably if you have your best talent write the Problem Specification. It will probably be called by another name, but you must insist that it describe (1) the overall problem, (2) the specific problem to be addressed by your program subsystem, and (3) how your subsystem is to interface with others. This difficult job demands your best people. They will usually be working as part of a team representing all the contractors and chaired by the customer or his representative.

Once you have an acceptable Problem Specification, you can operate in much the same way as described in the preceding chapters until you reach the Program Subsystem Acceptance Phase. You should insist on acceptance testing of your programs, even though acceptance this early will be conditional. Much may be expected to go haywire as you integrate your subsystem with the others later on. When the inevitable problems arise, it will be invaluable to you to be able to use those conditional acceptance tests as a baseline. If you leave them out, every problem that pops up is likely to produce a long wrangle going all the way back to who said what during the Definition Phase.

The System Test Phase in Figure 8.1 may be subdivided into a "laboratory" or "controlled" phase and a "live" or "field" phase. During laboratory system test, all subsystems are tied together at a special test facility before they are sent to a testing site where live conditions can be more closely approximated. As an example, if the system being developed is a ground-to-air missile weapons system, the program, computer, communications, radar, and missile subsystems may be integrated at the laboratory site and tested under partially simulated conditions. It will be necessary, however, to move to a remote live site in order to actually fire missiles at targets. Theoretically, all testing could be done at the live site, but this is usually not economically feasible because it might require large numbers of people and much extra equipment to be moved far away for long periods of time. By the time laboratory tests are completed, remaining problems will be minimal and fewer people will be required at the live test site.

The Site Installation and Test Phase acknowledges that even the live test site just mentioned may not be the last stop. Copies of the system may be sent to each of several geographic locations where they are finally to become operational. At these operational sites more tests will be run, once subsystems are adjusted for conditions peculiar to the individual sites. All this testing may, of course, take many months or even years, especially in an area as delicate as defense systems. During this time, project change control is especially important to prevent urgent field changes from contaminating the master copy of the system.

Organization

The basic organization in Figure 4.1b is still a good starting point, no matter how big the job is. As the number of people grows, however, more levels of management may be added. The positive side to this is that an adequate ratio of managers to programmers (or other workers) is maintained. The negative side is that there are now more communications problems and more fragmenting of the job.

In addition to the size of the job to be done, there are several kinds of functions that may cause growth in the project organization. One common requirement is the writing of the programming support tools to be used. You may not be programming a computer for which satisfactory support programs exist. You may need to write compilers, input-output packages, trace programs, special test aids, or even a complete "operating system." Since all this may easily be as big as the main job you are to do, you may find that you must add a big new box under the project manager called "support programming." (You must add a new section to your Project Plan to cover this effort.)

You may also have to account for "hardware diagnostics." By this I mean programs that exercise the hardware methodically in order to locate existing faults or attempt to predict imminent failures. Some computer manufacturers supply these programs with their hardware, but you may need to supplement them. You may even need to build an entire system of such diagnostic programs and tie them to the operational program system in such a way that they can be automatically invoked. Another box under the project manager!

All the other boxes in Figure 4.1b are likely to undergo a population explosion as you move from a medium-sized to a large project. The Staff Group will include more control functions, for example, "Configuration Management," and will be beefed up to handle more and bigger status reports and a great heap of other documentation. The Analysis and Design Group may have to grow in order to conduct myriad studies and to handle the layout of several different

versions of the evolving program system; this group may also do a lot
of simulation modeling. The Test Group's functions probably will
become much more critical in a big system as it becomes necessary
to do heavy testing of interfaces with other subsystems.

Customer Controls

Big projects mean big money and big money means people breathing
down your neck. The customer will insist on far more control over a
multimillion dollar project than over one having a modest price tag.
This is understandable, but what's distressing is the mountain of
paper accompanying these controls. For example, the United States
Government applies to many of its contracts a control scheme called
"Configuration Management." I'll define this in the next section, but
for now, take my word that it's a conceptually simple system: you
write a baseline definition of something to be built and control all
changes to those baselines. What could be simpler? But the mass of
manuals, regulations, specifications, and so on that has been built up
around that straightforward concept scares people to death. Whenever programmers hear "Configuration Management," they hide
behind the water cooler, because having seen the piles of manuals
and the endless forms, they want no part of them.

It's not that difficult. You can use Configuration Management on
your job very nicely if you can find someone who understands programming and programming management and who can write well.
Tell this person to do a translation job. Have him spend a month or
two learning the particular Configuration Management version that
your customer requires you to use. (There are at least three schemes:
Army, Air Force, and NASA. They're all alike conceptually, but
naturally different in implementation. Had they all been made exactly the same, many hundreds of government workers would be
out of a job!)

Now, once this person understands what's required, have him do
a translation *for your project*. The manuals and other descriptive
materials are written to cover all cases. All you need is something to
apply to *your* project. If the writer has the knack of boiling things
down to their essence, he will produce a guide for your organization
that will be about 5% the size of existing manuals.

There are other areas in which the customer may exert controls
beyond those applied to a smaller project. For instance, the customer
may insist on seeding some of your groups with his own people in
order to influence design, programming, and testing, as well as train

a cadre of people to eventually take over maintenance of the system. You may think all this a pain, but it need not be if you consider the following:

1. Try to have some veto power over the individuals the customer "lends" you. He may try to leave you with a few problem children. (Can't blame a guy for trying!)

2. Negotiate a clear understanding of your control over the customer's people — how long they are on loan to you, who manages them, and who appraises their work. On several jobs I know of, the people on loan were military men, some of whom left the job at critical times when their service hitches expired or when they were rotated to other areas.

3. Don't count one customer employee equal to one of your own and, therefore, reduce your manpower estimate accordingly. If your customer's employee turns out to be a dud, you're in trouble.

4. Don't assign one of the customer's people to a task on your "critical path."

Probably the best places to use customer personnel are in the analysis and testing areas, and in preparing user manuals. In analysis they should add their own unique understanding of the requirements of the job. In testing they may help you avoid later acceptance problems. And they obviously have a personal interest in writing good user documents.

Configuration Management

I've mentioned this concept several times. It's constantly changing and may be thrown out eventually in favor of a new system. What follows is based on the U.S. Army version of Configuration Management. It differs from other versions in details such as terminology, but not in concept.

The underlying idea of Configuration Management for programming is this: Define a program to be produced, control all changes to that original definition, and show that the final product is completely consistent with the original definition as modified by the accepted changes.

The basic unit of work to be controlled is called a Computer Program Configuration Item, or CPCI. A CPCI is a major piece of work, probably on the order of a subsystem, in the sense indicated in Figure 3.1.

Certain baselines are established for each CPCI. A baseline is anything that can be used as a departure point; it is what you and the customer agree will describe or constitute the product. Anything that later departs from a baseline is a change, and the change must be approved by the customer in advance. There are three baselines: (1) The "functional baseline," which is a description of the CPCI at a gross level, established at or before the beginning of the project; (2) the "allocated baseline," a more detailed description of the CPCI established during the Definition Phase; (3) the "product baseline," describing the CPCI after it has been built and tested. Each successive baseline becomes the new standard against which changes for that CPCI are judged.

A change to a baseline may be proposed by a member of the customer's organization, by you, or by any of the other contractors on the project. The formal change proposal document for most changes is called an Engineering Change Proposal, or ECP. (The term "engineering" reflects the fact that for many years Configuration Management was oriented solely around hardware.)

Each Engineering Change Proposal is brought before your Change Control Board (CCB), which consists of representatives from all major areas of your organization. The board's responsibility is to assure that the proposed change is sound and also to assess the impact, if any, on costs, schedules, and baselines. If there is an impact, the change is called "Class I," and it is sent to the customer's Change Control Board for its approval. When the customer sends back written approval, the change may be incorporated. For changes that your board feels will have negligible impact (called "Class II" changes), the change need not be approved by the customer. He is notified of the change, however, and does have the right to reclassify it as Class I.

Your Configuration Management staff keeps track of the status of each change for each version of the programs. The staff ensures that all necessary documentation changes are made and that the documentation and the programs are kept in step. At specified times the staff arranges for audits during which the consistency of programs and documentation is demonstrated to the customer.

Multiple Releases

On a big project there will usually be a need for more than a single version of the entire program subsystem. Three or more major versions, or "releases," are not uncommon for a project that spans several years.

The reason for multiple releases is that some systems are so technically difficult and so enormous in scope that they cannot be finished in a single development cycle. They require iteration, some trial-and-error, a careful building toward an ultimate system.

Multiple releases pose new management problems. How do you avoid endless confusion among the releases? A good way to start is by scheduling the beginning of work on each new release to coincide with the publishing of a new Problem Specification. If you plan three releases, plan three Problem Specifications, each one building on the preceding. Figure 8.2 shows a typical multiple-release schedule. Each black wedge represents publication of a new, more complete version of the Problem Specification. Each release bar represents a more or less complete program development cycle. The first release cycle may be abbreviated because the programs developed during that cycle may not be complete enough to subject to the final phases (full system testing and installation at an operational site).

The reason for keying the beginning of each new release cycle to the issuing of a new Problem Specification is that major changes in that specification on a weekly or monthly basis would make it nearly

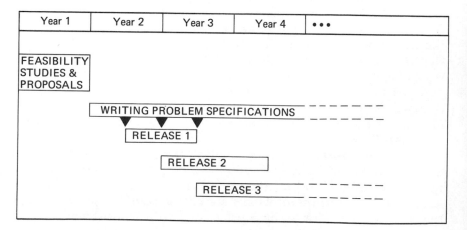

Figure 8.2. Scheduling multiple releases

impossible to produce *any* working version of the system. Instead, changes should be accumulated and issued in batches, that is, as part of the next scheduled Problem Specification.

Working on more than a single release at any given time makes manpower scheduling difficult. If there are three releases under way, it hardly seems reasonable to set up three complete organizations to produce them. Probably the best approach is to have a single Analysis and Design Group writing Problem and Design Specifications and to segment the Programming Groups.

SMALL PROJECTS

Many big projects could *be* small projects. If only we would stop building empires, we could do more jobs with excellence and stop spawning huge mediocrities. I don't know what that would do for unemployment, but it would surely make a *few* people happier and more productive.

The material in Chapters 1 to 7 still applies to those projects with only a handful of people, but, of course, the scope of things is different. You still need a Project Plan, although it may be but four pages long; you still need Problem, Design, and Coding Specifications; you still need to plan how to test your system. You need to do all the things that we've discussed if you're aiming to produce something of excellence. The difference lies in the amount of effort required. On the small project one person handles more than one job. Some tasks that consume great amounts of energy on big projects, for example, integration test, are accomplished in a breeze on small projects. And, of course, all that extra management and staff help needed on the big project just to handle the "bigness" and the inter-actions simply does not exist on the small job.

There is one danger on small projects that should be noted. The manager frequently gets sloppy in the control of a small task that requires perhaps six or eight people. There is the feeling that he is always on top of everything and nothing could possibly go wrong. A Design Specification doesn't get written, let alone a Problem Specification. Programs are not documented thoroughly because, after all, Charlie Programmer has the whole system in his head. So why insult Charlie by making him write it down? A Project Plan is obviously unnecessary — why write down a plan for an eight-person job? The manager who lets things go this way is begging for trouble, and when trouble comes, he will look far worse than the manager with the forty-person job who gets in trouble. It's *expected* that a competent manager can run the little job without bankrupting the company.

So, once again, pay attention to the advice given in earlier chapters and tailor it to your job. If you eventually want to manage a bigger project, do well on a small one first.

PROPOSALS

A proposal is your offer to do a job. Treat all proposals in life the same. Whatever you're saying when you're down there on your knees you may have to live with all your life. I've seen many proposals promise things that could not possibly be accomplished. Most of the time (but not always) these proposals are written by competent people who have good intentions.

I'm familiar with the arguments about how tough it is to write proposals: there's never enough time; the job description is vague; the RFP (Request for Proposals) is poorly written; adequate forces are not available; and on and on. It's true that writing proposals *is* tough; nevertheless, there are guidelines that can ease the task considerably.

1. *Be selective.* Don't write a proposal for every job in sight. Concentrate on the ones that you really want and do a first-rate job on them. One proposal guide observes:

   Many companies work on the basis that the number of contracts received will be in some ratio to the number of proposals generated. This is wrong. The number of successful proposals will be in direct relationship to careful proposal selection and preparation. A bad proposal is worse than none. First, it will not win. Second, it destroys the company's reputation and chances for the future. Third, it takes up the time of expensive talent and interferes with other work. . . . [*33*] .

2. *Cut out the baloney.* You're not kidding anybody by encasing three pages of good proposal work in a crust of garbage. Do you think proposal reviewers enjoy reading all that junk? Aim for a pithy piece of writing. Decide what you want to say, say it, and *stop!*

3. *Assign a proposal manager who has authority.* He should be able to make decisions fast and make them stick. There's no time for monkeying with a management chain a mile long.

4. *Make specific work assignments.* Assemble your people in a kickoff meeting, clearly state the objectives of the proposal task, and pass out the work. Some of the assignments will be investigatory; some will involve actually writing sections of the proposal. After people have had a chance to dig in for a couple of days, call another meeting and make any necessary adjustments to the assignments. As for *how* to make work assignments in the first place, I suggest you use the Project Plan outlined in Part II. Your proposal will have to contain most or all of the elements shown there. Why, half your job is already done for you!

5. *Outline the proposal.* Do this early. I've seen countless hours of work wasted because nobody bothered to outline the proposal document until late. Each one writes an out-line, injects his own style, organization, paragraphing, and so on — only to find that it doesn't mesh with anyone else's writing. Result: massive, wasteful rewrites. Settle the outline and writing guidelines *first* and avoid all that waste. Once again, the Project Plan outline in Part II may provide you with a good start at outlining the proposal document itself.

6. *Schedule the work.* Developing a proposal is, after all, a project. This project has objectives, deadlines, and limited resources. Schedule what must be done, when, and by whom. Schedule time for reviewing drafts and rewriting. Leave enough time for signoff and possible revision by upper management. And don't forget to allow sufficient time for technical editing, proofreading, final typing, reproduction, collating, and distribution of the finished copies.

7. *Don't be fast-talked into changing your estimates because they "won't sell."* If upper management decides to take a business risk by lowering your estimates, make your position clear. Don't, by your silence, give anyone the idea that you agree to the cut if you're actually opposed to it.

8. *State your assumptions.* When you submit to your management a finished proposal and a set of estimates, include in writing all assumptions that you made along the way, as well as your opinion of risks inherent in the estimates.

9. *Don't over-commit.* In most contracts the written proposal, unless amended by the contract, is considered a commit-

ment. If you promise more than you can deliver, you're likely to be stuck with that commitment.

10. *Be honest.* Proposals are big business. They are life and death ventures for many companies. The temptation to bend the truth, to use weasel words, to gloss over problems is sometimes overpowering. Many times I've heard an associate moan that "if we're completely honest about this estimate, we'll lose, because you *know* Company X isn't going to be honest about *its* estimate." Nuts! Resist that kind of thinking. Keep your integrity intact. You'll win in the long run.

Chapter 9

A War Story

The first version of this book was used extensively during the 1970s as a text or as required reading in many management classes. One of the comments I frequently heard was that the book would be more useful to teachers if augmented by case studies, questions and answers, or similar teaching aids. I answered that need, in the case of the first version, by writing and offering for sale a separate instruction package. It included a detailed course outline, a case study, class problems, visual aids, and teaching tips.

What follows is the essence of the case study included in that instruction package, but presented here more as a running story with frequent interruptions in order to pose some questions for you, the reader. I still offer the instruction package, now updated, for those interested, and it contains this story in case study format along with "answers" for the instructor's use.

This is the story of a real project, with names changed, as usual, to protect the guilty. I have taken liberties, made some changes, and left out a lot for the sake of clarity and brevity, but I've altered little concerning what actually happened on this project. As you read, put yourself in the place of the manager and consider how *you* might have handled things differently. Good luck!

NEW KID ON THE JOB

It's July 1. You've just been named to take over a new assignment. A major part of this assignment is that you become Project Manager on a job under contract to the U.S. Air Force. Your company, the ABC Corporation, has named this project FOUL, which stands for Follow-On, Unlimited.

During your first several days on the new job, you learn the following about Project FOUL:

- The contract is CPFF (Cost Plus Fixed Fee).

- The total period of performance is sixteen months.

- The system requirements were spelled out broadly in the RFP (Request For Proposals); a great amount of detail was to be supplied by the customer and documented by ABC during the course of the contract.

- The statement of work in the contract says essentially that (1) ABC will supply four of its standard Model T computers with specified configurations; (2) ABC will build a special display unit for attachment to each Model T; (3) ABC will write computer programs for this equipment to satisfy the system requirements; and (4) ABC will test and install all equipment and programs in four geographically separate locations: Washington, D.C., London, Hawaii, and Montana.

- The RFP describes the required system as a "command/control/communications system." The computers in London, Hawaii, and Montana are to digest data relative to their respective portions of the world entered via cards and punched paper tape. Each computer is to continually update its data base, update its displays, print reports for local military use, and pass on summary data to the central computer in Washington via low-speed data links. Depending on the nature of local input data, each area computer has several different levels of response-time requirements ranging from minutes to hours.

- The customer is to supply test time on the Model T situated in Washington, about thirty miles from ABC's offices. Access to this computer installation requires *secret* clearance.

- The contract calls for an immediate ABC staff of:

  one project manager
  one programming manager

    fifteen programmers
four system analysts
four special equipment engineers
one secretary

In addition, the customer is to supply four of his best available programmers to assist on the project under ABC direction.

- The proposal was written in four weeks by an ABC salesman, an ABC engineer who understood telecommunications equipment, an ABC programmer who had about four years' programming experience, and a programmer who had about two years' experience. Neither programmer knew anything about communications equipment.

PROJECT STATUS

During your first week on the project you find that:

- Although the project is six months old, staffing is incomplete.

	Proposed	Actual
Project manager	1	1
Programming manager	1	1
Programmers	15	6
System analysts	4	3
Engineers	4	4
Secretary	1	1
	26	16

- The detailed system requirements specifications are about one-third complete, according to the system analysts.

- Some programming has been done. A preliminary version of an executive control program is being tested. The programmers are working on various pieces of display programs, report programs, query programs, and message processing programs which apparently will all eventually be required.

- The more senior FOUL programmers are complaining that they don't really know what to program, because the requirements specifications are only one-third written. There is obvious tension between the analysts and the programmers.

- The analysts are edgy; they say that the requirements change every time they talk to the customer. The customer's reaction, according to your analysts, is that the requirements as stated in the RFP have not changed; they are merely being supplemented by the details which the contract called for.

- Until your arrival, the ABC salesman, on loan from the sales division, has been the acting Project Manager. He wants to return to full-time selling (to this and related customers).

- The salesman tells you that the customer has been irate over ABC's failure to staff the project as promised. He tells you that all attempts to find the people needed were frustrated by ABC's shortage of programmers and by mission squabbles among ABC managers. He assures you that the customer is now delighted because you and your programmers are on the scene.

- The present FOUL programming manager is the second person to fill the job. He, like his predecessor, wants to leave because he feels the changing requirements and the demanding customer are impossible to deal with.

- Three of the original FOUL programmers, all junior level, want out because they say they are doing nothing but "dog work." They have been converting a large data base from printed directories to punched-card formats for eventual inclusion into the system.

YOUR BACKGROUND

Before this assignment, you were a successful second-level programming manager. You had managed departments with as many as forty programmers, plus first-level managers, secretaries, and others. All previous jobs under you had been small and independent, no single job requiring more than six programmers. Most of your work had been of the "shop order" variety — that is, work done for other departments in ABC rather than for outside customers.

A major ABC reorganization broke up your old group and left you with twenty programmers, two first-level programming managers, a secretary, and a typist. All of your programmers and managers had had similar experience working on small, independent jobs. The experience mix is one programmer with eight years' experience, four programmers averaging four years' experience, and fifteen averaging one to two years.

YOUR JOB

The mission you accept when you take on your new assignment is bigger than Project FOUL. It is to build an ABC programming competence in the communications field. FOUL is simply the first job in that new field, and in fact the only one at present. The deadline for completing FOUL is next May 1, ten months away.

QUESTIONS

Your first week or so is taken up by the problems of the ABC reorganization, getting your people moved to a new building, and meeting the ABC people who have been working on FOUL. What you have learned about your new job is summarized in the preceding paragraphs. Most of your input has been verbal.

1. In what ways does your new assignment differ from your previous ones?

2. Should you accept the assignment as outlined, or would you attempt to redefine it?

3. During your next week on the job, what major actions will you initiate?

FIVE MONTHS LATER

The time is December 1. You have been on Project FOUL for five months. These are the highlights of what has occurred during your five months on the project:

- You appointed a design team of six people who produced an overall design for the program system in about two months (July and August). The design admittedly had some holes, but when it was presented to the customer he was pleased because it was the first such picture he had seen and he felt it a good start toward his final system.

- While the design team was at work (during those first two months) most of your remaining people were either attending classes or writing programs for FOUL, and were charging the contract. Four of your people were working on proposals unrelated to FOUL but bearing on your larger mission.

- When the design team finished work, you dissolved it and organized your people as shown in Figure 9.1. The numbers in parentheses represent numbers of people in each area.

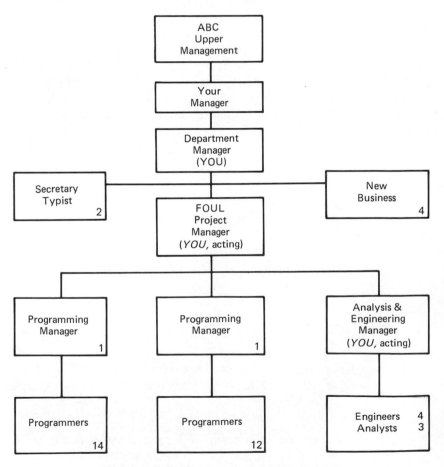

Figure 9.1. FOUL organization, September 1

- A contract change was negotiated in October covering all the people shown under the FOUL organization, Figure 9.1. The customer is so concerned about meeting the May 1 deadline that he is willing to pay for added people to get the job done.

Milestone number   1   2   3   4   5

	SEPT	OCT	NOV	DEC	JAN	FEB	MAR	APR
Factory test displays								
Ship to Washington								
Test displays with Model T								
Engineering documents								
Finish requirements specification								
Program subsystem A	(Detail design)			(Code & test)				
Program subsystem B	(Detail design)			(Code & test)				
Program subsystem C	(Detail design)			(Code & test)				
Program subsystem D	(Detail design)			(Code & test)				
System test						Prepare		
Field installation								
Descriptive documents								
User documents								
User training								

| | SEPT | OCT | NOV | DEC | JAN | FEB | MAR | APR |

Milestone Descriptions:

     1—Special display equipment shipped to Washington
     2—Requirements specs written and frozen
     3—System test begins
     4—System test ends
     5—End of contract

Figure 9.2. FOUL work schedule

- Having previously attended a Programming Project Management Course, you have learned the necessity for a set of documents called a Project Plan. There was no plan of much use when you joined the project, so you wrote one (with the help of your two programming managers) while the design effort was under way in July and August. The heart of your plan was the bar chart shown in Figure 9.2.

CURRENT SITUATION

As of December 1, you have the following problems:

- Detailed design on subsystems A, B, and C is not complete; you have a "gut feel" that D is also behind schedule.

- The requirements specifications are unfinished. The analysts complain that if the customer cannot be made to freeze the system, the requirements specifications will *never* be finished.

- The three programmers who wanted to leave the project when you first arrived (you talked them into staying) are again asking to get off the project. They have been joined by a fourth. All are from the original FOUL programming group. One of the four has suffered a nervous breakdown, requiring a one-month stay in the hospital. He blames his condition on the "impossible working conditions, the lack of direction, the long hours trying to meet management's unrealistic schedules, the obstinate customer."

- The customer has supplied his promised four programmers; two are assigned to each of your managers. Your managers' assessment is that one of them is equivalent to a good ABC junior programmer, and the other three have attended programming school but have no on-the-job experience.

- The customer has been asking for a month that you give him a detailed briefing on the status of the programming system. You have asked your programming managers to prepare for this briefing, but have met with a great deal of resistance because the managers don't want to waste their people's time in briefings. They feel that far too much of the programmers' time is already spent in meetings with the customer discussing changes and clarifications to requirements specifications, design documents, and so on. Besides, they say, it would take a great amount of time to prepare a comprehensive briefing because it would be necessary to reconstruct an overall design document. The one presented to the customer in September has not been kept current.

- One idea your managers see as a way of satisfying the customer is to list for him in detail all the program modules which have been completed. Since there are about seventy finished units, some of them integrated into larger packages, they feel such a listing should give the customer a secure feeling (and "keep him off our backs").

- On December 1 the customer insists in writing that you give him a full briefing on project status by December 15. He hints that any more foot-dragging will result in a call to the President of ABC. On the day the customer's letter arrives, you are out of town at another ABC installation with one of your programming managers looking into some possible shop-order work in support of your broader mission.

QUESTIONS

1. What do you do about the customer's request for a full briefing? Avoid it? Welcome it? Fake it?

2. List problems you feel exist as of December 1 and discuss possible solutions. Does your organization make sense? Your schedule? How comfortable are you with the various specifications? Are there any real alternatives to the May 1 delivery date?

HAPPY NEW YEAR

It's late December. You decided to give the customer the briefing he wanted. As a result of preparing for that meeting, you became absolutely convinced of the impossibility of meeting the May 1 deadline under any circumstances. In fact, your most optimistic completion date for any meaningful delivery is six months later than May 1, and even that date would require an immediate freeze on all changes. You tell this to the customer near the end of the briefing.

The customer is enraged and insists that ABC meet the May 1 deadline, no matter what the cost. He will cover all overtime expense, computer time costs, and so on. When you tell him that the job no longer can be finished by May 1 no matter what resources are applied, he demands and gets a meeting the next day with your manager and your manager's manager.

The meeting is reasonably calm. The customer reviews (1) ABC's performance on the contract, emphasizing late staffing; (2) ABC's complaints about what ABC calls "changes" but what the customer considers part of the job; (3) the extreme importance to the Joint Chiefs of Staff in meeting the May 1 date. Your management listens attentively and leaves, promising to meet again the next day with the customer to tell him what ABC is prepared to do. The customer smiles, shakes hands, and hopes he will not have to write that letter to ABC's President.

During a very late session that night attended by you, your subordinate managers, your manager, and his manager, the situation is summarized as follows by your manager's manager (who, incidentally, is a Vice-President of a major division of ABC):

1. The job this customer is trying to get done is obviously important to the government (although not of a critical emergency nature).

2. Good performance on this job is of crucial importance to ABC's hopes of getting a foothold in this expanding business area.

3. Since there are still more than four months to go, and since ABC has such great programming resources at its disposal, it should be possible through a crash effort to meet the May 1 deadline.

The Vice-President directs you to proceed with the job, holding May 1 as an inviolable deadline. To help you, he offers the following:

1. His assurance (he is backed by the Division President) that you will have available to you immediately any experienced

programmers or analysts you may select (or their equivalents) from anywhere within the Division. There are about a thousand programmers in the Division.

2. Authorization for all the paid overtime you can use.

3. Any assistance you may request from any of his staff.

As he prepares to leave the meeting, the Vice-President reminds you that, except for a few trivial items the customer has agreed to, you may not postpone or eliminate anything from the system. He also reminds you that he will not be available for the next day or so because of a huge problem at another location where a job has been cancelled and about five hundred ABC personnel are out of work.

QUESTION

You are still absolutely convinced of the impossibility of producing any working system by May 1. There is so much work to be done that no amount of added resources, in your opinion, can get the job done. What do you do about the Vice-President's demand? A time like this can be crucial to your career. What is your stand?

EPILOGUE

The Project Manager failed to say *no* to unreasonable demands in December. Out of a sense of pride, duty, allegiance (and with a liberal dose of hope), he decided to give May 1 a try. He found it impossible to look a Vice-President in the eye and say no.

May 1 was held as the final operational deadline and all else was based on the premise that that deadline could be met. Several steps were taken or attempted to help assure success.

1. All members of the project were authorized and directed to work the maximum amounts of overtime allowed by company regulations.

2. ABC management extracted a promise from customer management that the requirements would be frozen by February 1.

3. The Project Manager submitted in December a list of six top-notch ABC programmers to be immediately assigned to Project FOUL.

4. The Model T computer originally scheduled for Hawaii was ordered diverted and installed at the ABC FOUL work location for full-time use in testing FOUL programs.

5. All work not directly associated with FOUL was shelved.

6. A staff analyst was appointed as acting manager of the analysis and engineering group.

7. A junior programmer was given responsibility for controlling the use of the local computer.

8. Status meetings were to be held every Friday with the customer. A detailed listing of all program units was to be used as the reporting base.

Here is what resulted from each of the above actions:

1. Most of the programmers were already so worn out that the extra overtime produced no discernible improvement in their output. In a few cases the overtime was helpful for about two months. In other cases the overtime became "routine," and no more work was being accomplished than would have been done in straight time.

2. The customer finally froze the requirements specifications on March 15, six weeks before the system was to be finished and operational.

3. By January 15, one of the six programmers requested joined the FOUL project. A month later, a second man was signed up, but he was not one of the six requested. The Project Manager spent many days looking through personnel jackets and trying to get senior programmers who looked right for the job, but the net result was one of the six requested heroes and one substitute. All the others were unavailable because of their commitment to other jobs.

4. The Model T was successfully installed and in use by February 1.

5. All FOUL personnel were kept away from work not related to the project.

6. On March 15, after the customer had signed off on the requirements specifications and after all special engineering had been completed and documented, all the analysts and engineers except two were transferred to other jobs; the two remained to aid in the FOUL system test.

7. There was adequate computer time on the local Model T, but only by using a two-shift, seven-day operation. A problem arose in trying to transfer data from the customer's premises to the local Model T because some of the data were classified *secret*. The customer would not agree to allow the classified data to be used on the local ABC computer, no matter what security precautions were promised. By May 1 the FOUL programs were being tested first on the local ABC computer using simulated data, and then on the customer's machine using classified data. The two computers were in separate locations, about thirty miles apart.

8. The Project Manager reported each Friday on the status of program units (there were about 200 identified units). After the first few such status meetings, he found he was spending a larger and larger proportion of his time explaining why a unit reported as complete during a previous week was now being modified. The status reports more and more became exercises in tabulating numbers of units coded, assembled, and run successfully; percent of units completed; percent of units previously reported completed but now being modified; etc. The Project Manager felt like a statistician. By May 1 the weekly meetings became semiweekly.

By April it was understood by all that no system would be operational on May 1. System test had not begun, integration test was far from complete — how far, nobody was quite sure. There had been no formal recognition of the fact that May 1 would not be met, but conversations with the customer had begun to take on a tone of weary resignation, and the question became: "All right, ABC, when *will* you be finished?"

The answer was, almost a year later. There were several changes of management at ABC, including the Project Manager, his manager, and one of the programming managers. The customer was reasonably happy with the system that finally went on the air, patched though it was. The system cost several times its original estimate.

Most of the ABC people went on to other jobs, wiser for their experiences with FOUL. A couple checked into a rest home for tired managers. One wrote a book.

Chapter 10

A Summary

Here are some rules of behavior for successful project management:

Rule 1: Think "people" first, the business second. All a business *is* is its people. Take care of them.

Rule 2: Establish a clear definition of your project's development cycle and stick to it.

Rule 3: Emphasize the front-end of the project so that the rear-end won't be dragging.

Rule 4: Establish baselines early and protect them from uncontrolled change.

Rule 5: State clearly the responsibilities of each person on the project.

Rule 6: Define a system of documents clearly and early.

Rule 7: Never give an estimate or an answer you don't believe in.

Rule 8: Don't forget Rule 1.

Part II

A PROJECT PLAN OUTLINE

INTRODUCTION

The following pages suggest a format for a Project Plan. The Plan is divided into eleven sections; all sections except the last (Section 11, Index) follow the same broad outline:

SECTION n

n.1 OBJECTIVE

n.2 DISCUSSION

n.3 DETAIL

The first subsection (Objective) of each section should state clearly and briefly the intent of that section of the plan. I have included in the outline, *in italics*, my own concept of the objective of each section.

The second subsection (Discussion) should give the reader an understanding of the philosophy on which that section is based. The outline suggests, *in italics*, the kind of information appropriate to each section. This subsection should be tutorial. It should contain enough information so that the reader, by scanning only the Objective and Discussion subsections of the entire plan, can gain a good understanding of the plan without being smothered in details.

The third subsection (Detail) contains the guts of the plan. This subsection defines terms, tools, procedures, functions, responsibilities, schedules, and so on. Items in these subsections are discussed in appropriate chapters in Part I of this book. Again, some suggestions on content are included *in italics*.

Section I

Overview

1.1 OBJECTIVE

The objective of this section is to summarize the entire Project Plan.

1.2 DISCUSSION

Set the stage. Identify the customer and his experience in this field. Describe in one or two paragraphs the job to be done. Give any background necessary for a good understanding of the job environment. Then state your project's objectives under the contract.

Next, explain how the plan is organized. Promise the reader that he can gain a good understanding of the plan by reading each section's Objectives and Discussion, and then keep your promise.

Now list the assumptions and restrictions on which the plan is based. They're important. Don't hide them with a lot of words. State them honestly and simply.

Finally, establish a gross schedule for the project. This schedule should show all major efforts bearing on this project, whether under your control or not. For example, if other contractors are responsible for such tasks as writing specifications, developing hardware, or system testing, show all these efforts along with your own on a single diagram. If you're planning multiple releases, show how they are scheduled (see Fig. 8.2).

1.3 DETAIL

Give a brief statement of the objectives of each of the remaining sections of the plan.

Section 2

Phase Plan

2.1 OBJECTIVE

The objective of this section is to define the programming develop-ment effort in terms of a series of time-slices called "phases."

2.2 DISCUSSION

Define your development cycle and, briefly, each phase making up the cycle. Include an illustration such as Figure I or Figure 8.1 in Part I of this book, but include calendar dates. Establish basic defi-nitions and point out that the remaining sections of the plan are tied to these definitions. If you are planning multiple releases, show how they are scheduled in a series of overlapping, essentially identical, development cycles.

2.3 DETAIL

For each phase list primary and secondary objectives and define each objective as rigorously as possible.

2.3.1 Definition Phase
      2.3.1.1 Primary Objectives
            (a) Problem analysis

        (b) Detailed project planning
        (c) Defining acceptance criteria

2.3.1.2 Secondary Objectives
        (a) Finding people
        (b) Understanding the customer
        (c) Forming tentative design ideas

2.3.2 Design Phase

2.3.2.1 Primary Objectives
        (a) Baseline design for operational programs
        (b) Baseline design for support programs

2.3.2.2 Secondary Objectives
        (a) Preparation for integration testing
        (b) Setting up change controls
        (c) Constructing simulation models
        (d) Manning for subsequent phases
        (e) Preparation for programmer training
        (f) Publication of Programmer's Handbook
        (g) Initial preparation for system test
        (h) Initial preparation for acceptance test
        (i) Initial preparation for site test
        (j) Setting up project libraries

2.3.3 Programming Phase

2.3.3.1 Primary Objectives
        (a) Detailed design
        (b) Coding
        (c) Module test
        (d) Integration test
        (e) Program documentation

2.3.3.2 Secondary Objectives
        (a) Detailed preparation for system test
        (b) Detailed preparation for acceptance test
        (c) Detailed preparation for site test
        (d) Preparation for customer training

2.3.4 System Test Phase

2.3.4.1 Primary Objectives
        (a) Testing against Problem Specification
        (b) Testing as "live" as possible
        (c) Testing not controlled by programmers

2.3.4.2 Secondary Objectives
        (a) Completion of acceptance test preparations
        (b) Customer training

      (c) Correction oɪ descriptive documentation
      (d) Completion of user documentation
      (e) Reassignment of people

2.3.5 Acceptance Phase
    2.3.5.1 Primary Objectives
        (a) Execution and analysis of acceptance tests
        (b) Signing of formal acceptance agreement
    2.3.5.2 Secondary Objectives
        (a) Completion of customer training
        (b) Cleanup of documentation

2.3.6 Installation and Operation Phase
    2.3.6.1 Primary Objectives
        (a) Assistance in installing system
        (b) Assistance in beginning operation
    2.3.6.2 Secondary Objectives
        (a) Testing on-site
        (b) Continuing maintenance and tuning
        (c) Continuing operation
        (d) Project evaluation

Section 3

Organization Plan

3.1 OBJECTIVE

The objective of this section is to define the organization of the project and the assignment of responsibilities.

3.2 DISCUSSION

Review the basic reasons for establishing an organization: clarity of job assignment, minimizing interactions, controlling change, establishing points of responsibility and focus. Sketch the main flow of work within the organization, starting with problem analysis and design and running through programming, testing, documentation, and delivery.

3.3 DETAIL

In the first subsection list the groups which will be found on the organization charts and the general responsibilities of each group. Then show an organization chart for each phase. The organization will generally not be the same for all phases; for example, during the Definition Phase there will not yet exist a Programming Group.

3.3.1 Groups and General Responsibilities
     3.3.1.1 Analysis and Design Group
             (a) Writing Problem Specification
             (b) Writing Design Specification
             (c) Change control
             (d) Data control
             (e) Simulation modeling
             (f) Design and code inspections
             (g) Writing user documentation
     3.3.1.2 Programming Group
             (a) Detailed design
             (b) Coding
             (c) Module test
             (d) Integration test
             (e) Descriptive Documentation
     3.3.1.3 Test Group
             (a) Writing System Test Specifications
             (b) Writing Acceptance and Site Test Specifications
             (c) Validating test cases
             (d) Gathering and generating test data
             (e) Choosing and obtaining test tools
             (f) Setting up test libraries
             (g) Scheduling test resources
             (h) Executing tests
             (i) Analyzing test results
             (j) Documenting test results
     3.3.1.4 Staff Group
             (a) Library services
             (b) Computer time control
             (c) Supplying keypunch services
             (d) Planning and installing terminals
             (e) Issuing Programmer's Handbook
             (f) Training
             (g) Special technical assignments
             (h) Technical liaison
             (i) Document control
             (j) Report control
             (k) Contract change control
             (l) Supplying clerical support
             (m) Maintaining project history

3.3.2 Organization and Responsibilities:
     Definition Phase

3.3.3 Organization and Responsibilities:
Design Phase

3.3.4 Organization and Responsibilities:
Programming Phase

3.3.5 Organization and Responsibilities:
System Test Phase

3.3.6 Organization and Responsibilities:
Acceptance Phase

3.3.7 Organization and Responsibilities:
Installation and Operation Phase

Section 4

Test Plan

4.1 OBJECTIVE

The objective of this section is to define the tools, procedures, and responsibilities for conducting all levels of test of the program system.

4.2 DISCUSSION

A convenient way to write a test plan is to define each discrete level of test (for example, module test, integration test, system test, acceptance test, site test) and then describe the objectives, procedures, responsibilities, and tools for each level. In this subsection, briefly define each test level and show how the different levels fit together in a meaningful test hierarchy. Emphasize the need for modularity of the testing process and the need for certainty at one level before proceeding to the next.

4.3 DETAIL

4.3.1 Module Test
      Module test is testing done on the lowest-level program modules before they are integrated with other modules.
      4.3.1.1 Module Test Objectives
      4.3.1.2 Module Test Responsibility

4.3.1.3 Module Test Procedures
4.3.1.4 Module Test Entry Criteria
4.3.1.5 Module Test Exit Criteria
4.3.1.6 Module Test Tools

4.3.2 Integration Test
Integration test is the process of combining tested modules into progressively more complex groupings, either top-down or bottom-up, and testing these groupings until the entire program system has been put together and tested.
4.3.2.1 Integration Test Objectives
4.3.2.2 Integration Test Responsibility
4.3.2.3 Integration Test Procedures
4.3.2.4 Integration Test Entry Criteria
4.3.2.5 Integration Test Exit Criteria
4.3.2.6 Integration Test Tools

4.3.3 System Test
System Test is the retesting of the completed program system in as nearly a live environment as possible by personnel other than those who produced the programs.
4.3.3.1 System Test Objectives
4.3.3.2 System Test Responsibility
4.3.3.3 System Test Procedures
4.3.3.4 System Test Entry Criteria
4.3.3.5 System Test Exit Criteria
4.3.3.6 System Test Tools

4.3.4 Acceptance Test
Acceptance test is the exercising of the program system under conditions agreed to by the customer in order to demonstrate that the system satisfies the customer's requirements.
4.3.4.1 Acceptance Test Objectives
4.3.4.2 Acceptance Test Responsibility
4.3.4.3 Acceptance Test Procedures
4.3.4.4 Acceptance Test Entry Criteria
4.3.4.5 Acceptance Test Exit Criteria
4.3.4.6 Acceptance Test Tools

4.3.5 Site Test
Site test is testing of the program system in its ultimate operating environment to assure readiness for operation.
4.3.5.1 Site Test Objectives
4.3.5.2 Site Test Responsibility

4.3.5.3 Site Test Procedures
4.3.5.4 Site Test Entry Criteria
4.3.5.5 Site Test Exit Criteria
4.3.5.6 Site Test Tools

4.3.6 Common Test Facilities
Describe the facilities and tools common to several or all levels of test.
4.3.6.1 Development Support Library
4.3.6.2 Computer Facilities
4.3.6.3 Keypunch Services
4.3.6.4 Terminal Systems
4.3.6.5 Operating Systems
4.3.6.6 Special Languages
4.3.6.7 Test Run Pickup and Drop Areas

4.3.7 Testing Support Programs
Describe anything unique about the testing of the test tools themselves.

Section 5

Change Control Plan

5.1 OBJECTIVE

The objective of this section is to define the procedures to be used for controlling change in the evolving program system.

5.2 DISCUSSION

Describe the customer's need to know that what is being developed by you is what was envisioned when the contract was signed, and your own need for knowing that what the programmers are producing is what was originally intended. A solution to this problem is to establish certain critical baseline documents acceptable to both customer and you, and to control events always relative to those baselines. Whenever a question is raised, the baseline documents are the reference point. Anything anyone wants that is not covered in the baselines is a change, and it must be negotiated. When a change is deemed necessary, its cost and impact, if any, must be assessed, and the change must be written into the baseline document(s). A revised baseline document becomes the new baseline.

5.3 DETAIL

5.3.1 Baselines
Define the documents to be used as baselines on your project.

5.3.1.1 Problem Specification
5.3.1.2 Design Specification

5.3.2 Proposing a Change
5.3.2.1 Who May Propose a Change
   (a) Project members
   (b) Customer
   (c) Other contractors
5.3.2.2 Change Proposal Document

5.3.3 Investigating a Proposed Change
5.3.3.1 Who, How, When
5.3.3.2 The Investigator's Report
   (a) Summary of proposed change
   (b) Originator's name and organization
   (c) Classification of the change
   (d) Impact on costs, schedules, other programs
   (e) Recommendations

5.3.4 Types of Changes
5.3.4.1 Type 1
   The change affects a baseline or would cause a cost, schedule, or other impact.
5.3.4.2 Type 2
   The change affects no baseline and has negligible cost, schedule, or other impact.

5.3.5 Change Control Board
5.3.5.1 Membership
5.3.5.2 When It Meets
5.3.5.3 How It Operates

5.3.6 Types of Recommendations
5.3.6.1 Acceptance
5.3.6.2 Rejection

5.3.7 Implementing a Change
5.3.7.1 Estimating Cost of Change
5.3.7.2 Approvals
   (a) Project management
   (b) Customer
5.3.7.3 Documenting the Change
5.3.7.4 Testing the Change

Section 6

Documentation Plan

6.1 OBJECTIVE

The objective of this section is to define the procedures and resources required for the publication cycle and to outline a basic set of project documents.

6.2 DISCUSSION

Emphasize that all project documents will be outlined in this section and no new kinds of documents are to be written unless management can be shown why the currently planned documents are inadequate; in that case, a new document will be outlined and added to the plan. Include a chart such as that shown on p. 223 summarizing the Documentation Plan and complete with details peculiar to your job.

6.3 DETAIL

6.3.1 Publication Procedures
      6.3.1.1 Preparation and Approval
      6.3.1.2 Typing
            (a) Manual
            (b) Semi-Automatic

6.3.1.3 Proofing and Editing
6.3.1.4 Reproduction
    (a) Routine
    (b) Bulk
6.3.1.5 Distribution
    (a) Within the project
    (b) To the customer
    (c) Other contractors
    (d) Company management
    (e) Vital records storage

6.3.2 Project Documents
This subsection outlines a number of basic project documents. You may need to delete certain of them or add others: you will also probably change titles by inserting your project name or abbreviation. The outlines follow.

PROBLEM SPECIFICATION

DOCUMENT NUMBER:

APPROVALS:

DATE OF ISSUE:

SECTION 1: SCOPE

The Problem Specification describes the "why" of the project and the requirements of the program system, that is, the job to be done by the programs. It is a baseline document and its most recent edition is to be adhered to strictly by all project personnel.

SECTION 2: APPLICABLE DOCUMENTS

SECTION 3: REQUIREMENTS

This section, the heart of the document, states in as much detail as possible the job the programs are to do. Almost all of the information here will be some combination of narrative description, mathematics, and tabular data. HIPO charts and data flow diagrams are also used to express required functional relationships, but not program logic design.

3.1 Performance Parameters

This subsection spells out the system's requirements for transaction rates, throughput, etc., as imposed by the problem environment. These requirements may be stated in terms of file capacities, acceptable timing constraints, permissible input rates, and so on. These requirements are stated in quantitative terms, with tolerances where applicable.

3.2 Operational Requirements

This subsection shows the functional requirements of the program system. The intent is to show all functional operations of the programs, the relationships among those functions, and the tie-in between program functions and other subsystem functions. Each program function is further defined in separate subsections as shown below.

3.2.1 Function 1

3.2.1.1 Source and Type of Inputs
3.2.1.2 Destination and Type of Outputs
3.2.1.3 Functional Diagram

3.2.n Function n

3.2.n.1 Source and Type of Inputs
3.2.n.2 Destination and Type of Outputs
3.2.n.3 Functional Diagram

3.3 Data Requirements

This section defines data parameters that affect the program system design, for example, geographic coordinates for operational sites. The detailed definition of parameters includes descriptions of the data, definitions of units of measure, and accuracy and precision requirements.

3.4 Human Performance

This section describes requirements involving human interactions with the program system, such as minimum times for decisions, maximum times for system responses, restrictions on program-generated displays.

DESIGN SPECIFICATION

DOCUMENT NUMBER:

APPROVALS:

DATE OF ISSUE:

SECTION 1: SCOPE

This document defines a solution to the problem described in the Problem Specification. The Design Specification is the foundation for all program implementation. The design logic described here is detailed enough so that all required functions are satisfied, and all interfaces, system files, and the logic connecting all program modules are defined. The design is done in sufficient detail that all system logic problems are resolved and the complete program system "hangs together." The lowest level of program module is specified in terms of the functions it must perform and the interfaces it must have with other modules, but the actual internal design of these lowest-level modules is left to the implementing programmers.

If the project is to produce more than one program system, for example, support programs in addition to operational programs, there will be more than one Design Specification.

SECTION 2: APPLICABLE DOCUMENTS

SECTION 3: OVERALL DESIGN CONCEPT

This is an overview of the entire program system design at a high level.

3.1 Program Hierarchy

Definition and description of the program system hierarchy.

3.2 Data Hierarchy

Definition and description of the system files and their interrelationships, including simple pictures of file structures.

3.3 Standards and Conventions

3.3.1 Design Standards and Conventions

Definition of all standards and conventions adopted for use in this design document and to be observed during later detailed design.
3.3.1.1 HIPO Standards
3.3.1.2 Flow Chart Standards
3.3.1.3 Naming Standards
3.3.1.4 Interfacing Standards
3.3.1.5 System Macros
3.3.1.6 Message Formats

3.3.2 Coding Standards and Conventions

Definition of all standards and conventions to be observed during coding.
3.3.2.1 Languages

3.3.2.2 Prohibited Coding Practices

3.3.2.3 Required Coding Practices

3.3.2.4 Recommended Coding Practices

SECTION 4: THE BASELINE DESIGN

This is the focal point of this document. All program and system file logic is presented here to the level of detail the designers feel is necessary before turning the document over to the programmers for implementation.

4.1 Program Design

4.2 File Design

Pictorial layouts of all system files describing all subdivisions of the files and characteristics of those subdivisions, such as field lengths and identifying characters. Also, a complete description of the relationships among the various files, including pointers used to link files and coverage matrices showing which programs access each file.

SECTION 5: DATA FLOW

This section uses flow diagrams and accompanying narrative to describe the major transactions in the system, irrespective of the actual logic structure of the system. The intent is to provide an understanding of data paths and major events in the operational system, including all subsystems, hardware as well as software. This exposition is useful as an introduction to the system and should not presume programming knowledge on the part of the reader. (See description of data flow diagrams in Chapter 3.)

CODING SPECIFICATION

DOCUMENT NUMBER:

APPROVALS:

DATE OF ISSUE:

SECTION 1: SCOPE

A standard statement: This document contains the detailed description of program module _____ ."

SECTION 2: APPLICABLE DOCUMENTS

A standard statement keying this detailed specification to the appropriate part of the Design Specification: "The design described in this document represents that portion of the baseline design shown in the Design Specification, document number _____ , subsection _____ ."

SECTION 3: THE DETAILED DESIGN

3.1 Program Structure

This section describes the logic of the program module according to the standards and conventions adopted and stated in the Design Specification, subsection 3.3.

3.2 File Structures

3.2.1 System Files

This subsection makes explicit references to the system file layouts contained in the Design Specification. File layouts may be repeated here if the programmer feels this would enhance the clarity of this document.

3.2.2 Local Files

A complete, detailed description of all local files. Local files are unique to this program module. They are not accessed by other modules.

SECTION 4: LISTINGS

This is a standard reference to the detailed, machine-produced instruction listings showing the complete set of object code for this module, including any local files.

CHANGE PROPOSAL

DOCUMENT NUMBER:

DATE OF ISSUE:

ORIGINATOR'S NAME:

ORIGINATOR'S ORGANIZATION:

SECTION 1: PROPOSED CHANGE

SECTION 2: NEED FOR THE CHANGE

SECTION 3: IMPACT

A brief discussion of the cost of making the change, as far as the originator can determine. This section is optional.

ATTACHMENTS: SUPPORTING MATERIALS

Papers, listings, etc., which help to explain the problem and the proposed solution.

PROBLEM SPECIFICATION CHANGE NOTICE

DOCUMENT NUMBER:

APPROVALS:

DATE OF ISSUE:

SECTION 1: SCOPE

A brief summary of a change to the current Problem Specification. All Change Notices are distributed to all holders of the Problem Specification.

SECTION 2: INSERTIONS AND DELETIONS

A list showing which pages in the current Problem Specification are to be removed, and which new pages are to be inserted.

ATTACHMENTS:

All new pages to be inserted into the Problem Specification.

DESIGN SPECIFICATION CHANGE NOTICE

DOCUMENT NUMBER:

APPROVALS:

DATE OF ISSUE:

SECTION 1: SCOPE

A brief summary of a change to the current Design Specification. All Change Notices are distributed to all holders of the Design Specification.

SECTION 2: INSERTIONS AND DELETIONS

A list showing which pages in the current Design Specification are to be removed, and which new pages are to be inserted.

ATTACHMENTS:

All new pages to be inserted into the Design Specification.

TEST SPECIFICATION

DOCUMENT NUMBER:

APPROVALS:

DATE OF ISSUE:

SECTION 1: SCOPE

There are four separate sets of test specifications: Integration, System, Acceptance, and Site Test Specifications. The outlines for all four are identical, except that the appropriate qualifier ("integration," "system," "acceptance," or "site") must be inserted. The content of the specifications may, of course, vary considerably, although two of them (acceptance and site) will often be identical. This section, Scope, should serve in each case as an introduction to the document, describing its intent and how it is to be used.

SECTION 2: APPLICABLE DOCUMENTS

SECTION 3: (INTEGRATION, SYSTEM, ACCEPTANCE, SITE) TEST OVERVIEW

3.1 Testing Philosophy

3.2 General Objectives

3.3 General Procedures

3.4 Success Criteria

SECTION 4: COVERAGE MATRIX

A chart listing along the vertical axis the areas to be tested and along the horizontal axis the test case number(s) covering each area. When complete, this chart amounts to a cross-reference between all areas to be tested and all test cases covering those areas.

TEST CASE

TEST CASE NUMBER:

APPROVALS:

DATE OF ISSUE:

SECTION 1: BACKGROUND

1.1 Objectives

1.2 Assumptions

1.3 References

(Including required user documents).

1.4 Success Criteria

SECTION 2: DATA

Identification and description of the data to be used in the test.

2.1 Simulated Input Data

2.2 Live Input Data

2.3 Predicted Output Data

SECTION 3: SCRIPT

The step-by-step instructions for conducting the test. The script lists procedures (actions to be taken by the testers) down the left half-page and leaves space for comments to be written in along the right half-page. The script answers the following questions:

1. *What is to be done?*
2. *By whom?*
3. *When to do it?*
4. *What to look for?*
5. *What to record?*

SECTION 4: CHECKLISTS

Checklists appropriate to this test case to aid in posttest analysis.

TEST REPORT

TEST CASE NUMBER:

The test report may refer to either an integration, system, acceptance, or site test; the report title should be filled in accordingly. But no matter which type of test is involved, the report is keyed to a unique test case number.

APPROVALS:

TEST DATE:

REPORT DATE:

NAME OF TEST CONDUCTOR:

PROBLEMS ENCOUNTERED:

If no problems, so state. Otherwise, each identifiable problem is listed on a separate sheet attached to this cover sheet. For each problem, the following information is to be given:

1. *A unique problem identification number using the test case number as a base.*

2. *Identification of the program modules in which the problem occurred, if known.*

3. *A description of the problem, with all available supporting data.*

4. *Recommendations, if any, for possible solutions to the problem.*

TECHNICAL NOTE

DOCUMENT NUMBER:

APPROVALS:

DATE OF ISSUE:

TEXT:

These are documents such as working papers and technical ideas—anything of a technical nature not explicitly covered by another document. They may be generated by anyone. The only control over them is that each is assigned a unique number, as is any other document, and each is filed in the project library.

ADMINISTRATIVE NOTE

DOCUMENT NUMBER:

APPROVALS:

DATE OF ISSUE:

TEXT:

These are documents conveying nontechnical information, for example, announcements, minutes of meetings, organizational changes. Some Administrative Notes are simply cover sheets for such documents as contract changes. Each note is assigned a unique document number and is filed in the project library.

PROGRAMMER'S HANDBOOK

DOCUMENT NUMBER:

SECTION 1: INTRODUCTION

1.1 Objectives

The Handbook is intended to be the source of basic technical information required by all programmers on the project. The information in the Handbook is to be considered "law" until a change is approved and distributed.

Strictly speaking, the Handbook is not a single document, but a collection of documents that every programmer on the project should have close at hand. It is extremely important that the Technical Staff (responsible for issuing and updating the Handbook) not allow additional materials to be added randomly. Otherwise, the Handbook will grow large and unwieldy and will simply gather dust.

The Handbook is in loose-leaf notebook form in order to facilitate updates. It is divided into sections with a major tab for each, and subtabs where appropriate.

1.2 Scope

The Handbook should be restricted to the topics listed in this outline. There is a great deal of information pertinent to the project (plans, status reports, etc.) that is not included. Keep the Handbook concise and usable from the programmers' point of view.

1.3 Publication

Initial distribution is made near the end of the Design Phase. Subsequent updates are made in two ways:

1. Routine weekly update.

2. Emergency 24-hour update.

In either case, updates are handled in this manner:

1. *Anyone drafts an update.*
2. *Technical Staff gets the draft typed, proofread, approved, reproduced and distributed.*

SECTION 2: THE PROBLEM

2.1 Introduction

A tutorial description of the customer, the environment, and the job to be done. This should start from scratch and be written so that a new project member can easily know what the job is all about. The limit should be about two pages.

2.2 The Problem Specification

The entire Problem Specification is included here.

SECTION 3: TESTING

The entire Test Plan is included here.

SECTION 4: SUPPORT PROGRAMS

Descriptions of the programming tools available to the programmer, and how to use them. Each main category of tools should be separately tabbed within this section.

SECTION 5: THE DESIGN SPECIFICATION

The entire Design Specification is included here. This document contains several main subsections each of which should be given separate tabs in the Handbook. The subsections are: Overall Design Concept; Design Standards and Conventions; Coding Standards and Conventions; The Baseline Design.

SECTION 6: DOCUMENTATION

6.1 Documentation Summary

A chart similar to that on p. 223 is included here.

6.2 Documentation Tools

Tools such as an automatic flowcharter are described here.

6.3 Documentation Index

A detailed, cross-referenced index of all project documents, updated weekly.

NAME OF DOCUMENT	CONTENTS	PREPARATION			APPROVAL		DISTRIBUTION	
		WHO WRITES	WHEN FINISHED	FORMAL PROOFING, EDITING BY TECH PUBS	WHO APPROVES THIS DOCUMENT	CUSTOMER FINAL APPROVAL TIME (CALENDAR DAYS)	WHO GETS	NO. OF COPIES
PROBLEM SPECIFICATION	A description of the requirements of the problem to be fulfilled by the Program System	Analysts	End of Definition Phase	Yes	Customer			
DESIGN SPECIFICATION	A description of the design to be used by the programmers in producing the Program System	Analysis and Design Group	End of Design Phase	Yes	Customer			
CODING SPECIFICATION	A detailed description of the modules produced by the programmers; in toto, these specifications describe the complete Program System	Individual programmers	Preliminary version at end of module test; final version at end of acceptance test	Yes	Customer			
CHANGE PROPOSAL	A description of a proposed change to the Problem Specification and/or the Design Specification	Anyone	Anytime	No	Nobody			
PROBLEM SPECIFICATION CHANGE NOTICE	A description of adopted changes to the current Problem Specification	Contractor's Analysis and Design Group	Anytime	No	Contractor Customer			
DESIGN SPECIFICATION CHANGE NOTICE	A description of adopted changes to the current Design Specification	Contractor's Analysis and Design Group	Anytime	No	Depends on change			
INTEGRATION TEST SPECIFICATION	A description of the philosophy, objectives, and procedures involved in integration test; a matrix of test cases	Programmers	End of Design Phase	No	Contractor			
SYSTEM TEST SPECIFICATION	A description of the philosophy, objectives, and procedures involved in system test; a matrix of test cases	Test Group	End of Programming Phase	No	Contractor			
ACCEPTANCE TEST SPECIFICATION	A description of the philosophy, objectives, and procedures involved in acceptance test; acceptance criteria; a matrix of test cases	Test Group	Preliminary version end of Definition Phase; Final version, end of Programming Phase	Yes	Customer			
SITE TEST SPECIFICATION	A description of the philosophy, objectives, and procedures involved in site test; a matrix of test cases	Test Group	End of Programming Phase	Yes	Customer			
TEST CASE	Individual test script and data	Test Group and Programmers	Depends on type of test	No	Depends on type of test			
TEST REPORT	A report of any problem encountered during any formal test; integration, system, acceptance, site	Test Conductor	After running any test cases	No	Nobody			
TECHNICAL NOTE	Miscellaneous technical correspondence	Anyone	Anytime	No	Depends on content			
ADMINSITRA-TIVE NOTE	Miscellaneous administrative correspondence	Anyone	Anytime	No	Depends on content			
PROGRAMMER'S HANDBOOK	Collection of data needed by the programmer	Technical Staff	First version at end of Design Phase	No	Contractor			
TECHNICAL STATUS REPORT	A single form used in reporting technical status to the next higher management level within the contractor's organization	Each level	Biweekly or monthly	No	Nobody			
PROJECT HISTORY	A set of charts showing • significant events • manpower (estimated vs. actual) • machine time (estimated vs. actual)	Administrative Staff	At end of contract	No	Contractor			
DOCUMENTA-TION INDEX	Listing of all current project documents	Administrative Staff	Published periodically	No	None			

Documentation summary

SECTION 7: EQUIPMENT

A description of the operational and support hardware to be used on the project, complete to the level of detail required by the programmers. The kinds of information included are:

1. *Gross diagrams showing main elements of the hardware and their interconnections.*

2. *More detailed diagrams describing individual hardware subsystems.*

3. *Tabular data needed by the programmer, such as input-output timing characteristics, data transfer rates, storage capacities, character sets.*

SECTION 8: GLOSSARY

Definitions of project terms, including the names of program levels and testing levels, customer jargon, equipment nomenclature.

TECHNICAL STATUS REPORT

DOCUMENT NUMBER:

DATE OF ISSUE:

WORK PACKAGE NUMBER(S):

ASSIGNED TO:

DESCRIPTION OF TASK:

A single descriptive sentence.

END DATE:

When the task is scheduled to be finished.

STATUS:

Both a qualitative and quantitative assessment.

PROBLEMS:

PROJECT HISTORY

DOCUMENT NUMBER:

APPROVALS:

DATE OF ISSUE:

SECTION 1: SCOPE

A general statement telling the reader the intent of this document. It is a historical record of important events and data on the project for use in planning and estimating later phases of the project or entirely new projects. It is intended to be a crisp summary, not a huge collection of paper.

SECTION 2: SIGNIFICANT EVENTS

A chronological listing and very brief summary of important events during the life of the contract, including missed milestones, new estimates, contract changes, project reviews, equipment installation dates, important telephone agreements, meetings with the customer, and meetings with subcontractors, team members, or vendors.

SECTION 3: MANPOWER HISTORY

Charts showing three major items:

1. *Total estimated manpower (in man-months) at the beginning of the contract in each of the categories listed in Figure 2.7a.*

2. *A record of changes in the estimated numbers shown in (1) and notations explaining the reasons for the changes.*

3. *Total manpower actually used during the contract in each category listed in (1).*

Comparison between (1) and (3) should be very helpful in future estimating, provided the figures in (2) are taken into account.

SECTION 4: MACHINE TIME HISTORY

A series of charts similar to the manpower history. Keep one chart for each type of machine used. Each chart shows:

1. *Total hours estimated for this machine at the beginning of the contract in these categories:*
       module/integration test
       system test

acceptance test
other

2. *A record of changes in the estimates shown in (1) and notations explaining the reasons for the changes, including differences between expected and actual configurations.*

3. *Total machine time actually used during the contract in each category listed in (1).*

A postmortem comparison between (1) and (3), taking (2) into account, should assist in future estimating.

DOCUMENTATION INDEX

DOCUMENT NUMBER:

DATE OF ISSUE:

This is an index of all current project documents. It is maintained in computer storage for quick updating and frequent printing. This index is a chart with the following column headings:

1. *Document number*

2. *Document title*

3. *Date of issue*

4. *Author (if appropriate)*

Section 7

Training Plan

7.1 OBJECTIVE

The objective of this section is to define the contractor's training responsibilities.

7.2 DISCUSSION

The programming contractor is responsible for two general categories of training: internal (training his own people) and external (training the customer, the system contractor, and others).

7.3 DETAIL

7.3.1 Types of Training
      7.3.1.1 Internal Training
          (a) Understanding the overall project
          (b) Technical
- coding languages
- use of test tools
- use of terminals
- the data processing hardware
- interfacing with other subsystems
- the problem
- the baseline design

(c) Nontechnical
- management techniques
- change control procedures
- documentation control
- reporting requirements
- clerical procedures

7.3.1.2 External Training
(a) Installing the program system
(b) Using the system
(c) Modifying the system

7.3.2 Resources
For each type of training identified show:

- *training schedules*

- *instructors required*

- *training materials*

- *facilities (classrooms, computers, etc.)*

- *numbers of trainees*

- *special computer programs for training*

Section 8

Review and Reporting Plan

8.1 OBJECTIVE

The objective of this section is to describe the means of reviewing and reporting progress.

8.2 DISCUSSION

There is informal review and reporting going on at all levels more or less continuously. This plan addresses not the informal, but rather the formal reviewing and reporting. This Discussion subsection should describe in a general way the reporting structure. It should stress the importance of making financial and technical reports consistent with one another. It should describe the contractor's accounting system to which the project's financial reports must conform (see Fig. 4.6).

8.3 DETAIL

8.3.1 Reviews
    8.3.1.1 Internal Reviews
        Participants in each internal review include project members and outside reviewers.
        (a) Definition Phase Review

When: End of Definition Phase
Objectives: To review the Problem Specification and determine readiness for the Design Phase; to review and assess the Project Plan; to review acceptance criteria.

(b) Preliminary Design Review
When: Midway in the Design Phase
Objective: To review the baseline design, as far as it has been developed, in order to assure the validity of the design approach.

(c) Design Phase Review
When: End of Design Phase.
Objectives: To review the completed Design Specification to determine whether or not it satisfies the Problem Specification and is reasonable and programmable; to review the Project Plan. **Include outside reviewers.**

(d) Programming Phase Review
When: End of Programming Phase.
Objectives: To review program integration results and determine readiness for the System Test Phase; to review program documentation.

(e) System Test Phase Review
When: End of System Test Phase.
Objectives: To review system test results and determine readiness for the Acceptance Phase; to review program documentation.

(f) Postmortem Review
When: End of Acceptance Phase.
Objective: To review and approve the Project History document.

8.3.1.2 External Reviews
Participants in each of these reviews include representatives of the contractor and the customer.

(a) Preliminary Design Review
When: Midway in Design Phase, after internal review.
Objective: To review the validity of the design approach.

(b) Design Phase Review
When: At the end of the Design Phase, after internal review.

Objectives: To review in detail and concur on the Design Specification; to review the contractor's Project Plan in preparation for entering the Programming Phase.

(c) Acceptance Review

When: End of Acceptance Phase.

Objective: To review the results of the completed acceptance tests and determine any remaining problems that must be corrected before the customer will formally accept the programs.

8.3.1.3 Structured Walk-Throughs

These are held whenever there is a product (a design, code, test plan, user's manual, anything) ready for a close look by other project members guided ("walked through") by the developer of that product. The objective is to find errors, not to report status.

8.3.2 Reports

8.3.2.1 Generated by Nonmanagers

(a) Frequency: *bi-weekly.*

(b) To: *immediate manager.*

(c) Format: *Technical Status Report (see Documentation Plan).*

(d) Scope: *one report for each task assigned.*

8.3.2.2 Generated by Managers

(a) Frequency: *bi-weekly.*

(b) To: *immediate manager.*

(c) Format: *Technical Status Report.*

(d) Scope: *one report for each milestone task.*

8.3.2.3 Generated by Project Manager

(a) Frequency: *monthly and quarterly. A quarterly report should replace the monthly report normally due at that time.*

(b) To: *company management and customer.*

(c) Format: *depends on company and customer requirements, but should include these types of information:*
- *technical status of major tasks*
- *milestones met*
- *milestones missed; why; remedial action*
- *significant problems*
- *financial status, expenditures vs. budget*

8.3.2.4 Generated by Company Staff

Describe reports fed back to management by the company. These reports are usually financial and might include actual cost information for the current week, actual vs. budget data for the current month, and a picture of the project's overall financial status thus far.

Section 9

Installation and Operation Plan

9.1 OBJECTIVE

The objective of this section is to define the contractor's responsibilities in installing and operating the accepted program system.

9.2 DISCUSSION

The amount of participation by a contractor in installing and operating a system he has delivered is a variable from one project to the next. In this Discussion subsection, describe the degree of this involvement for your project.

9.3 DETAIL

9.3.1 Installation
    9.3.1.1 Responsibility
    9.3.1.2 Schedule
    9.3.1.3 Conversion
        (a) Method
            Parallel operation, immediate replacement, etc.
        (b) Cutover criteria
            How the decision is to be made to cut off the old system and rely on the new.

Section 10

Resources and Deliverables Plan

10.1 OBJECTIVE

The objective of this section is to gather in one place a summary of all resource estimates and a schedule for all deliverables.

10.2 DISCUSSION

Various resources, schedules, and deliverable items are mentioned or implied in other sections of the Project Plan. Here they are all tied together and made explicit.

10.3 DETAIL

10.3.1 Manpower
A chart showing total manpower planned for the project on a monthly basis. A main chart should show two broad categories: programming and nonprogramming manpower. Included in the first are programmers and their first-level managers; in the second are all other kinds of manpower. Supporting charts should break down the two categories into more detail.

If the project is large and if there are a number of major program subsystems, show separate manpower charts for each. Examples of major subsystems might be: an "operating system"; tactical programs; support programs; maintenance and diagnostic programs.

If the project plans a number of releases of the complete program system, show manpower for each release separately.

10.3.2 Computer Time

Show monthly computer time requirements broken down by program release, by major program subsystem within release, and by use category: module/integration test, system test, acceptance test, site test. If more than one type of computer installation is used (for example, contractor's facility, customer's facility) show separate estimates. Show computer time separately for other categories, such as project administrative uses.

10.3.3 Other Resources
    10.3.3.1 Publications Costs
        (a) Reports
        (b) Problem Specification
        (c) Design Specification
        (d) Coding Specifications
        (e) User documents
        (f) Test documents
    10.3.3.2 Travel Costs
        (a) To contractor's own facilities
        (b) To customer facilities
        (c) To other contractors' facilities
        (d) To test sites
    10.3.3.3 Relocation of Employees and Equipment
    10.3.3.4 Equipment and Supplies
        The normal office equipment and supplies plus any special items, such as extra keypunches, automated typing terminals, extra diskettes, tapes, and so on.
    10.3.3.5 Special Purchases or Rentals
        Such items as extra office space or temporary quarters in trailers.

10.3.4 Delivery Schedules

Chart(s) showing dates for all deliverables called for in the contract or in any subsequent agreements; accompanying the chart should be a set of narrative capsule descriptions of each item shown on the chart.

10.3.5 Milestones Chart

A chart showing all milestones against which reports to the customer are to be made. A good base for this chart would be a variation of Figure I. It's helpful to show milestones overlaid on a development cycle, so that one can better relate each milestone to the planned major activities, that is, the phases. Include a separate sheet giving a capsule description of each milestone indicated on the chart. Figure 2.5 will give you a start at developing your set of milestones.

10.3.6 Budget

A copy of the financial budget showing how funds are allocated to each of the cost categories shown in preceding sections. As estimates are reconsidered and changed, the budget must change. When that happens, this subsection must be updated to reflect the change.

Section II

Project Plan Index

This is simply a conventional index of major subjects to help the reader find topics he or she wants within the Project Plan. A few hours' attention to an index will render the entire plan much more useful.

Bibliography and References[1]

1. Lt. Col. John Manley, USAF, "Embedded Computer System Software Reliability," *Defense Management Journal,* October 1975, p. 18.

2. Robert Townsend, *Up The Organization* (New York: Alfred A. Knopf, Inc., 1970), p. 36.

3. Reprinted by permission from *Programming Project Management Guide,* International Business Machines Corporation, 1970.

4. Many of the items listed in Figure 2.8 are reproduced from tables contained in E. A. Nelson, *Management Handbook for the Estimation of Computer Programming Costs* (Santa Monica, Calif.: System Development Corporation, 1967).

5. Robert Gunning, *The Technique of Clear Writing* (New York: McGraw-Hill, 1968), p. 259.

6. Joseph Orlicky, *The Successful Computer System* (New York: McGraw-Hill, 1969), p. 113.

7. Joseph Orlicky, *The Successful Computer System* (New York: McGraw-Hill, 1969), p. 111.

8. Joan Hughes and Jay Michton, *A Structured Approach to Programming* (Englewood Cliffs, N.J.: Prentice-Hall, 1977), pp. 70–78.

9. P. Van Leer "Top-Down Development Using a Program Design Language," *IBM Systems Journal,* 15, no. 2 (1976), pp. 155–170.

[1] These entries are listed in order of their appearance in the text.

10. For a comprehensive coverage of programming languages see Jean E. Sammet, *Programming Languages: History and Fundamentals* (Englewood Cliffs, N.J.: Prentice-Hall, 1969).

11. J. F. Stay, "HIPO and Integrated Program Design," *IBM Systems Journal*, 15, no. 2 (1976), pp. 143–154.

12. Joan Hughes and Jay Michton, *A Structured Approach to Programming* (Englewood Cliffs, N.J.: Prentice-Hall, 1977), pp. 6–8, 56–60.

13. Harlan D. Mills, "Software Development," *IEEE Transactions on Software Engineering*, SE-2, no. 4 (December 1976).

14. Clement McGowan and John Kelly, *Top-Down Structured Programming Techniques* (New York: Petrocelli/Charter, 1975), pp. 97, 125–132, 148.

15. Edward Yourdon, *Techniques of Program Structure and Design* (Englewood Cliffs, N.J.: Prentice Hall, 1975), pp. 59–74, 259–263.

16. F. Terry Baker, "Structured Programming in a Production Programming Environment," *IEEE Transactions on Software Engineering*, SE-1, no. 2 (June 1975).

17. A. M. Pietrasanta, "Managing the Economics of Computer Programming," *Proceedings of the 23rd National Conference, Association for Computing Machinery*, 1968, pp. 341–46.

18. Churchman, Ackoff, and Arnoff, *Introduction to Operations Research* (New York: Wiley, 1957), pp. 411–14.

19. Edward Yourdon, *Techniques of Program Structure and Design* (Englewood Cliffs, N.J.: Prentice-Hall, 1975), p. 144.

20. Joan Hughes and Jay Michton, *A Structured Approach to Programming*, (Englewood Cliffs, N.J.: Prentice-Hall, 1977), p. 3.

21. Richard C. Linger, Harlan D. Mills, and Bernard I. Witt, *Structured Programming: Theory and Practice* (Reading, Mass.: Addison-Wesley, 1979), p. 1.

22. Corradò Böhm and Guiseppè Jacopini, "Flow Diagrams, Turing Machines, and Languages with Only Two Formation Rules," *Communications of the ACM*, 9, (May 1966), pp. 366–371.

23. M. E. Fagan, "Design and Code Inspections to Reduce Errors in Program Development," *IBM Systems Journal*, 15, no. 3, 1976, pp. 182–211.

24. J. D. Aron, "The Superprogrammer Project," in *Software Engineering Techniques*, ed. J. N. Buxton and B. Randell (NATO Scientific Affairs Division, Brussels, 1970), pp. 50–52.

25. F. T. Baker, "Chief Programmer Team Management of Production Programming," *IBM Systems Journal*, 11, no. 1 (1972), pp. 56–73.

26. F. T. Baker, "System Quality Through Structured Programming," in *Proceedings. AFIPS 1972 FJCC*, 41 (Montvale, N.J.: AFIPS Press 1972), pp. 339–343.

27. Clement McGowan and John Kelly, *Top-Down Structured Programming Techniques* (New York: Petrocelli/Charter, 1975), pp. 144–162.

28. Edward Yourdon, *Techniques of Program Structure and Design* (Englewood Cliffs, N.J.: Prentice-Hall, 1975), pp. 85–86.

29. Robert Townsend, *Up the Organization* (New York: Alfred A. Knopf, Inc., 1970) p. 11.

30. Ned Chapin, "New Format for Flow Charts," *Software Practice and Experience*, 4, no. 4 (Oct. to Dec. 1974), pp. 341–347.

31. Charles P. Lecht, *The Management of Computer Programming Projects* (New York: American Management Association, 1967).

32. Robert Townsend, *Up the Organization* (New York: Alfred A. Knopf, Inc., 1970), p. 37.

33. Paul R. McDonald, *Proposal Preparation Manual* (Covina, Calif.: Procurement Associates, 1968).

34. C. Kreitzberg and B. Schneiderman, *The Elements of FORTRAN Style* (New York: Harcourt Brace Jovanovich, 1971).

35. Edward Yourdon, *Techniques of Program Structure and Design* (Englewood Cliffs, N.J.: Prentice-Hall, 1975), p. 57.

36. W. P. Stevens, G. J. Meyers, and L. L. Constantine, "Structured Design," *IBM Systems Journal*, 13, no. 2 (1974).

37. Frederick P. Brooks, Jr., *The Mythical Man-Month: Essays on Software Engineering* (Reading, Mass.: Addison-Wesley, 1975).

38. Gerald M. Weinberg, *The Psychology of Computer Programming* (New York: Van Nostrand Reinhold Company, 1971).

39. Joel D. Aron, *The Program Development Process* (Reading, Mass.: Addison-Wesley, 1974).

40. D. L. Parnas, "On the Criteria to Be Used in Decomposing Systems into Modules," *Communications of the ACM*, 15, no. 12 (1972).

41. H. D. Mills, "Human Productivity In Software Development," an unpublished paper, 1976.

Index